# Collected Poems

# Collected Poems

## Louis Simpson

**PARAGON HOUSE**
*New York*

First paperback edition 1990

**Published in the United States by**

Paragon House
90 Fifth Avenue
New York, NY 10011

Copyright © 1988 by Paragon House Publishers

A signed, limited edition is available.

*The Best Hour of the Night* by Louis Simpson. Copyright © 1983 by Louis Simpson. Reprinted by permission of the publisher, Ticknor & Fields, a Houghton Mifflin Company.

*Caviare at the Funeral* by Louis Simpson. Copyright © 1980 by Louis Simpson. Reprinted by permission of the publisher, Franklin Watts.

*A Dream of Governors* by Louis Simpson. Copyright © 1959 by Louis Simpson. Reprinted by permission of the publisher, Wesleyan University Press.

*At the End of the Open Road* by Louis Simpson. Copyright © 1963 by Louis Simpson. Reprinted by permission of the publisher, Wesleyan University Press.

"Searching for the Ox" reprinted by permission of *The New Yorker*.

*Searching for the Ox* by Louis Simpson. Copyright © 1976 by Louis Simpson. Reprinted by permission of the publisher, William Morrow & Co.

10  9  8  7  6  5  4  3  2

Library of Congress Cataloging-in-Publication Data
Simpson, Louis Aston Marantz, 1923–
    Collected poems.
    Includes indexes.
    I. Title.
PS3537.I75A6  1988      811'.54      88-9879
ISBN 1-55778-047-1
1-55778-156-7 (limited edition)
1-55778-411-6 (pbk.)

Manufactured in the United States of America

This book is dedicated to my mother,
Rosalind de Marantz Barsanti

# Contents

*These are the poems I would like to be remembered by. The title of each book is followed by poems selected from that book.—LS*

*Preface*     *xiii*

*The Arrivistes: Poems 1940–1949*    1949

| | |
|---|---|
| Allan Fox | 3 |
| Jamaica | 5 |
| The Warrior's Return | 7 |
| Roll | 8 |
| Arm in Arm | 9 |
| Lazarus Convalescent | 10 |
| Invitation to a Quiet Life | 11 |
| Summer Storm | 13 |
| A Witty War | 14 |
| Why This? | 15 |
| Room and Board | 16 |
| The Protestant | 17 |
| Laertes in Paris | 18 |
| Yes Yes | 21 |
| Resistance | 22 |
| Carentan O Carentan | 23 |
| Song: "Rough Winds Do Shake the Darling Buds of May" | 25 |
| The Arrivistes | 26 |

*Good News of Death and Other Poems*    1955

| | |
|---|---|
| The True Weather for Women | 47 |
| As Birds Are Fitted to the Boughs | 48 |
| A Woman Too Well Remembered | 49 |
| The Man Who Married Magdalene | 50 |
| The Window | 51 |
| Memories of a Lost War | 52 |

The Battle                                          53
The Heroes                                          54
The Ash and the Oak                                 55
American Preludes                                   56
West                                                59
Early in the Morning                                60
Aegean                                              61
Mississippi                                         62
Islanders                                           63
Good News of Death                                  67


*A Dream of Governors*  1959
The Green Shepherd                                  81
I Dreamed that in a City Dark as Paris              83
A Dream of Governors                                84
Orpheus in the Underworld                           86
The Flight to Cytherea                              88
To the Western World                                90
Hot Night on Water Street                           91
The Boarder                                         92
Orpheus in America                                  93
An American in the Thieves' Market                  95
Music in Venice                                     96
Côte d'Azur                                         98
The Runner                                          100
Old Soldier                                         124
The Bird                                            125
The Silent Generation                               129
The Lover's Ghost                                   130
The Goodnight                                       131


*At the End of the Open Road*  1963
In California                                       135
In the Suburbs                                      136
The Redwoods                                        137
There Is                                            138
Summer Morning                                      140
Birch                                               141

The Morning Light                                        142
The Cradle Trap                                          143
A Story about Chicken Soup                               144
The Troika                                               145
New Lines for Cuscuscaraway and
    Mirza Murad Ali Beg              146
Moving the Walls                                         147
Frogs                                                    151
My Father in the Night Commanding No                    152
American Poetry                                          154
The Inner Part                                           155
On the Lawn at the Villa                                 156
The Riders Held Back                                     157
A Farm in Minnesota                                      159
Love, My Machine                                         160
Wind, Clouds, and the Delicate Curve
    of the World                     161
Walt Whitman at Bear Mountain                            162
Pacific Ideas—A Letter to Walt Whitman                   164
Lines Written Near San Francisco                         165

*Selected Poems*  1965
The Union Barge on Staten Island                         171
Columbus                                                 172
The Laurel Tree                                          174
Things                                                   177
Outward                                                  179
Stumpfoot on 42nd Street                                 180
After Midnight                                           182
Luminous Night                                           183

*Adventures of the Letter I*  1971
Dvonya                                                   187
A Son of the Romanovs                                    188
Meyer                                                    190
The Country House                                        191
A Night in Odessa                                        192
Isidor                                                   193

Adam Yankev                                    194
Indian Country                                 196
The Climate of Paradise                        198
On the Eve                                     199
The Wall Test                                  200
American Dreams                                201
Doubting                                       202
The Pihis                                      204
The Photographer                               205
Simplicity                                     206
Vandergast and the Girl                        208
On a Disappearance of the Moon                 210
Port Jefferson                                 211
Island                                         212
A Friend of the Family                         213
The Foggy Lane                                 217
Sacred Objects                                 218
Today                                          220
Yen Yu                                         221
Love and Poetry                                222
Trasimeno                                      223
The Peat-Bog Man                               224
The Silent Piano                               225

*Searching for the Ox*   1976
Venus in the Tropics                           229
Dinner at the Sea-View Inn                     231
The Psyche of Riverside Drive                  233
Lorenzo                                        236
The Stevenson Poster                           240
The Hour of Feeling                            242
The Sun and the Moon                           244
The Mannequins                                 245
The Middleaged Man                             246
Newspaper Nights                               247
Baruch                                         248
Mashkin Hill                                   251
Searching for the Ox                           252

A Donkey Named Hannibal                        257
The Street                                     258
Big Dream, Little Dream                        259
Before the Poetry Reading                      260


*Caviare at the Funeral*   1980
Working Late                                   265
New Lots                                       266
Sway                                           269
On the Ledge                                   272
A Bower of Roses                               274
American Classic                               277
Little Colored Flags                           278
The Beaded Pear                                279
The Ice Cube Maker                             282
Magritte Shaving                               283
A River Running By                             284
An Affair in the Country                       286
The Old Graveyard at Hauppauge                 287
Unfinished Life                                288
Why Do You Write about Russia?                 292
Typhus                                         295
The Art of Storytelling                        296
The Pawnshop                                   297
Caviare at the Funeral                         298
Chocolates                                     299
The Man She Loved                              300
Peter                                          302
Maria Roberts                                  303
Armidale                                       305
Out of Season                                  310
The Mexican Woman                              313
Back in the States                             314


*People Live Here: Selected Poems 1949–1983*   1983
The Fleet for Tsushima                         317

*The Best Hour of the Night* 1983
    Physical Universe    321
    How to Live on Long Island    324
    Encounter on the 7:07    326
    Damned Suitcase    331
    Quiet Desperation    333
    The Previous Tenant    336
    The Eleventh Commandment    350
    Periodontics    352
    Ed    356
    Bernie    357
    Elegy for Jake    359
    Akhmatova's Husband    362
    Red-Avoiding Pictures    363
    The Champion Single Sculls    364
    A Fine Day for Straw Hats    365
    A Remembrance of Things Past    367
    The Gardener    369
    Reflections in a Spa    370
    In Otto's Basement    371
    In a Time of Peace    372
    The Unwritten Poem    374

*Index of Titles*    375
*Index of First Lines*    381

# Preface

I PUBLISHED MY FIRST BOOK when I was twenty-six, paying the printer myself. This was in Paris. I carried the galleys back to my hotel in Rue Jacob, passing a bookstore on the way. The owner was at the door, looking into the street. I had spoken to him once or twice and was so happy to have the galleys of my book that I showed them to him. "What is it?" he said. I told him, my poems. He took the galleys from my hand and tossed them in the air. They were heavy and fell with a thud. "Poetry," he said, "should float. It should fly." This was my first meeting with a critic.

The reader who begins at the beginning will see my faults clearly enough. I have not tried to rewrite and improve the early poems—such attempts, I think, are always unsatisfactory. Better to let one's past alone and leave it to others to judge . . . I may have changed the spelling of a word, or the punctuation, but that is all.

The forms of my writing have changed considerably since *The Arrivistes*, but the themes have been fairly consistent. I once arranged my poems under these headings: The Fighting in Europe, A Discovery of America, Modern Lives, Tales of Volhynia, and Recapitulations. The poems about war emerged from my experience as an American soldier in the Second World War. In the second category were poems in which I attempted to understand my adopted country—I was not born in the United States but came here when I was seventeen.

Under Modern Lives I placed poems that described human situations—poems with people in them. I am particularly fond of the narrative element in poetry—in fact can hardly enjoy a poem that is all idea and has no visible place or action.

My mother was born in Russia. She emigrated to the United States as a young girl, became an actress, and travelled to Jamaica to make a movie. There she met my father. He was a lawyer and we lived as people of the professional class did in the colonies, taking our ideas from England. My mother was the embodiment of a different way of life entirely, exotic and romantic. The poems about Volhynia are based on stories she told me and, years later, my reading of Russian authors.

Last, under Recapitulations . . . poems that draw disparate experiences together and attempt to bring order out of chaos. I have always felt that there is a power and intelligence in things. I felt it as a boy when I watched the sun setting from the top of a mountain, when I rode a bicycle in the lanes of Kingston or walked along the shore, listening to the sea. I felt that power when I first saw Manhattan rise out of the Atlantic, the towers a poet describes as "moody water-loving giants." During the war I felt there was an intelligence watching and listening.

Or were we listening to one another? When I came upon an old trench of the First World War I remembered the lines by Wilfred Owen:

> Our brains ache, in the merciless iced east winds
>      that knive us . . .
> Wearied we keep awake because the night is
>      silent . . .

Weeks later, in the snow around Bastogne, I could apply these words to myself and my companions. Poetry speaks from one generation to another, yet speaks to the individual as though it were meant for him or her alone.

In recent years I have written about occurrences, sometimes very ordinary ones, in which there is a meaning hidden beneath the surface. Bringing out such meanings, it seems to me, is a road poetry can take in a world that, as it grows more industrial, seems less beautiful in the old sense. The more banal and "anti-poetic" the material, the more there is for the poet to do. For this work a sense of humor is as necessary as an awareness of the drama, the terror and beauty of life.

# The Arrivistes
## Poems 1940–1949
### 1949

# Allan Fox

After the show the silver stars were out
In multitudes, but not such platitudes
Had medicined to that sleep Sundays owe . . .
For this was Sunday, quiet and so strong,
The time when spacious nostrils, breathing long,
Cooled down the fiery days.

The taxi pounces at the crossing ways
And to the music of the horn they go
Between the pews of green lights row on row.
Now the towers hold their priestlihood
In iron perpendiculars. Late hours
Are lonely. There are few things so alone
As empty streets with one illumined window
Hinting at people dancing to and fro
Around the phallic phonograph. He said
'Twas time for little girls to be in bed.

Bessie, the sheets were cold.
I think the streets are cold.
True, there's nothing colder than a street
But I feel so romantic at dead-ends,
I feel like crying Jesus come to me.
But cops would come to me . . . my destiny.

Mr. Allan Fox inside his dream
Saw many soldiers,
Shellshatter, and a vision
Of private tombs. Her blond hair on the stone
He kissed again; he held her tenderly
And pressed the dry bones to him lovingly.

He startled out of sleep, then, deeply moved,
Got up and washed his face. The morning came
Across Manhattan like a smoky flame.
He turned from washing to the one he loved
Saying Alice
Alice you must go now.
So I left by the back door, Bessie.

3

On Mondays all the world is born again,
The subways move against oblivion,
I, Allan Fox, am sensitive to things
I would not change my destiny with kings.
Each blade in Central Park renews life's promise . . .
He thinks of Sundays and he thinks of Alice
And happily he walks on, and he sings.

# Jamaica

Far from your crumpled mountains, plains that vultures ponder,
White gulches, wounded to pythons from gunshot of thunder:
        What should I sing in a city of stone,
        Drawing the bow across skull, across bone?

On phosphorescent furrows drifting from the dark sand,
We felt the fish pluck, keel grate, were laughed at by the land,
        Saw searchlights comb corpses' hair in mangroves
        Malarial, birds beat to quiet coves.

The gull shuddered plashing from sharks; and under green
   glass
Delicate needles to death twitched in terror's compass;
        Crimson on blue blade, gaping like hooked gills
        The sun was drawn bleeding across the hills.

By the sunk schooner, the nets, canoes with broken backs,
Was a cathedral, now choral to currents: now shacks
        Show a negress, children swollen with gas,
        A man cuts coconuts with a cutlass.

This island seemed emerald in the steel furnace flame
To the pirate . . . Port Royal . . . his ship shed clothes as she came
        To lie in the bay's blue arms, lazy, lean,
        And gold glowed through the hull with a death sheen.

He lay on shore with a black and a gold-hearted girl
Whose laugh unhinged like a box of red velvet and pearl.
        She gave his enemies the Judas word
        Who came at cock-crow, each one with a sword.

Still she cherished in womb the chromosomes for whiteness.
Fish flittered about the father's bones, but she could press
        Her hands to the high jumper there, the warm
        Mulatto, ambitious in lizard form.

This got the start of my bestial, indolent race
With coarse skin, crazy laugh, nostrils like swords through
   the face:
        Athletes at sixteen, they dive deep and lie
        In women like waves: in such dark caves die.

Bitter pale beauty, the small salty jewels of sun
Fade by the ocean. But the fruit of the valleys run
        From plump bourgeois banana's yellow skin
        To the cruel cane, cutlass-bladed, thin.

Life is a winter liner, here history passes
Like tourists on top-decks, seeing the shore through sun-
    glasses:
        And death, a delightful life-long disease,
        Sighs in sideways languor of twisted trees.

# The Warrior's Return

Oh strict society, bright town
Whose towers never tumbled down,
Whose pigtails never caught on fire:
Call Odysseus a liar!

Allan Fox surveyed his city
With a soldier's trained self-pity.
To polished pavements, shining shoes
He offered only the excuse
"At war, sir, in another country."

I saw him in a dirty dive
Dead drunk to prove he was alive,
And every time it wagged, his tongue
Surprised him, such sad songs it sung.
And at his sorrow I stood sentry . . .

»Dans une guerre de Jules Verne
J'ai trouvé une machine
Pas du tout compliquée . . .
Elle avait sa combine.

»Les beaux jours sont partis.

»A l'hôpital,
Loin du caporal,
J'ai longtemps regardé
Mes pieds gelés.

»Après, Place Pigalle
Sous la Cathédrale
Elle a fait pour Papa
Ce qui est principal . . .

»Le bien et le mal.»

# Roll

What, my friends! Dead only two years and already dumb?
Must we hang your skulls in the square?
You've acres enough. Move over and give us your graves.

Two years since Utah and already lost your voices . . .
So silent, you skeleton stoics?
Here rentals are rising: how is it in your neighborhood?

Oh when you were men, so far better soldiers than I,
I was watching your faces to learn.
But they were so many, how can I remember them all?

They call to the companies: will you rise to the roll . . .
To Russia, wherever, laughing
Again to be marching, again to be going to war?

"Why am I here?" said one on the way to his death.
I would bring him a wreath, but fear
Rousing his wrath. I'd say more, but my tongue is no
      trumpet.

# Arm in Arm

Arm in arm in the Dutch dyke
Were piled both friend and foe
With rifle, helmet, motor-bike:
Step over as you go.

They laid the Captain on a bed
Of gravel and green grass.
The little Dutch girl held his head
And motioned us to pass.

Her busy hands seemed smooth as silk
To a soldier in the sun,
When she gave him a jug of milk
In which his blood did run.

O, had the Captain been around
When trenching was begun,
His bright binoculars had found
The enemy's masked gun!

Beside a Church we dug our holes,
By tombstone and by cross.
They were too shallow for our souls
When the ground began to toss.

Which were the new, which the old dead
It was a sight to ask.
One private found a polished head
And took the skull to task

For spying on us . . . Till along
Driving the clouds like sheep,
Our bombers came in a great throng:
And so we fell asleep.

9

# Lazarus Convalescent

These are the evening hours and he walks
Down to the Hudson, to that lonesome river,
And while a piano plays he sits and talks . . .
"Do you remember Judson?
Huge cloudy symbols of a high romance.
I think he went into insurance."

The water laps, the seagulls plunge and squawk
And lovers lock in wind that makes him shiver.
"I'll have to learn to use a knife and fork
Again. Look there above us!
Spry's for Baking . . . starry spectacle.
For Frying. More, a miracle."

Perhaps at running water he can balk
The bloodhound that is howling for his liver.
Now will he rise again, rise up and walk.
"And do you know, I've found
My neighbors spy on me when I undress.
Perhaps I ought to change, to change my address."

He sees his oracle, the weight machine.
His flesh is right; he laughs and pats the giver.
Alas, its entrails also tell his fortune,
Turning him ghastly white.
He moves from all his friends with a cursed stealth.
What has the mouth informed him? "Guard your health."

# Invitation to a Quiet Life

Come, Amaryllis, let us go
To see the moving picture show
Where the small people, closely pressed,
Walk all together in their best.
The angels and a taxi shall
Take us to Times Square. From his stall
The cripple sells us several views
Of what is playing. Let us choose
Some gay melodic musical . . .
But first, flock to the seasonal

Sheep-shearing in the Great White Way
Where thousands sacrifice their pay
In groves to oracles, and pass
Gazing at goddesses in glass.
Here every Beauty on parade
Compares the compromise she's made,
And former school-friends when they meet
Look down and fidget on their feet.
Then, Amaryllis, we shall be
Equal to our society.

A sultan's story-telling wife
Once played a one-night stand for life . . .
These Scherezades sing to please,
Showing their talent or their knees.
One thousand nights, and if she cracks
What does an actress get? The axe.
Here Cinderella, pumpkin tripper,
Tosses now a married slipper;
She strides her bar-stool like a throne.
The wicked sisters drink alone.

Since sin requires some expense
Our income is our innocence.
We gain, but then we borrow more,
Become dependent on the law,
(Like lilies clothed, like pigeons fed)
We woo and by installments wed.

In penny arcades, bowling, beer
And dancing we shall pass the year.
Then, Nymph with inky fingertips,
Type me six copies of your lips.

Some day we'll poster in a plane
To the Bahamas or to Maine,
And pat the minutes with our hands
Into castles on the sands,
Watching white argosies of gulls
And the long shark haunt the hulls,
And split with springing steel a log
To the approval of the dog,
Grow ever greener in the Greek
Religion of a good physique.

It seems the gentle and the human
Become an office man or woman,
And hundreds at the Hudson stand
Who've lost hereditary land
Not by a Mississippi flood
But in a slower sea of mud.
Youth fades, the hockey-hero's laugh
Is fixed as in a photograph . . .
Forgotten what enormous rage
Bore us like soldiers to the stage.

Since, Amaryllis, you and I
Adore an advertising sky
And find it happiness to stare
At the enchantments of thin air,
Let us go in, and not regret
The endings that we never met,
But in security applaud
The ecstasies we can't afford.
So shall we manage, till the day
Death takes the furniture away.

# Summer Storm

In that so sudden summer storm they tried
Each bed, couch, closet, carpet, car-seat, table,
Both river banks, five fields, a mountain side,
Covering as much ground as they were able.

A lady, coming on them in the dark
In a white fixture, wrote to the newspapers
Complaining of the statues in the park.
By Cupid, but they cut some pretty capers!

The envious oxen in still rings would stand
Ruminating. Their sweet incessant plows
I think had changed the contours of the land
And made two modest conies move their house.

God rest them well, and firmly shut the door.
Now they are married Nature breathes once more.

# A Witty War

Oh, we loved long and happily, God knows!
A witty war that flourished seven years,
Where the small river to the ocean flows.
Our quarrel made us kiss, kisses brought cares,
And closeness caused the taking off of clothes.
Oh, we loved long and happily, God knows!

—"The watchdogs are asleep, the doormen doze!"
We made our own sweet music on the stairs.
Lightly we stepped and little stood to lose;
We had our own, and the world its, affairs . . .
Or so we said while taking off our clothes.
Oh, we loved long and happily, God knows!

Between us two a silent treason grows.
Our eyes are empty, or they meet with tears.
Wild is the wind, from a cold country blows,
In which our tender greenness disappears.
And did this come of taking off our clothes?
Oh, we loved long and happily, God knows!

The bells beginning gladly, at the close
Tongue sullenly. Your jetty shining hair
And your brown eyes would be the worst of foes,
For they know when to strike my heart and where.
This nakedness is all our own, God knows,
And shall remain till time makes us some clothes.

# Why This?

Why this?
        Not for the fame, for I have lost
My shirt, that was as white as any shroud,
And will not go to dinner like a ghost
To be a silly cipher to the crowd.
No, I have come into a quiet coast
Where only what's most human is allowed:
Clear air and water, meat, a roof and post,
And speech, for I can only live aloud.

And I've found nothing better, to be brief,
Than you. And knowing that we daily die
I wish to set in order my belief,
Which is these articles: a bugle eye,
Your cheeks of cream, arms, knees, etcetera,
Of which I'll make an item every day.

# Room and Board

The curtained windows of New York
Conceal her secrets. Walls of stone
Muffle the clatter of the fork.
Tomorrow we shall see the bone.

In silence we construct a sect . . .
Each of us, comrades, has his own.
Poems that will not take effect,
Pictures that never will be known.

The landlord wipes his mouth of pork,
Pauses to eavesdrop, disconnect
The water and the telephone;

And Death's unmarried daughter crawls
Along the thin lath of the walls
And knocks, because we live alone.

# The Protestant

The gray roof of Saint Germain,
The craters of the moon,
Regard the drunken Protestant
Who hums a dying tune.

Left right left the students go
The communistic street
Bras dessus bras dessous,
The priest calls to his cat.

Nor Church nor State shall save his life,
The women know his price,
Who tried to lead a decent life
Of intermittent vice.

His heart pounds to the Métro gate,
He holds his ticket out
And staggers forward, but too late.
The gate grinds firmly shut.

One arm upon the rail, and one
Palm upward in the dirt . . .
Heel on his neck, Parisian,
And someone steal his shirt!

The Protestant pink elephant
Shall never graze upon
The gray roof of Saint Germain,
The craters of the moon.

# Laertes in Paris

## I

Decades of disaster, a deluge . . .
Helmets glimpsed in battle on the plain . . .
Back to Paris for a kindly refuge
You come, demoralized and drenched again,
With your poetic soul like a black dog.

The old cathedrals, comfortably huge,
Loom up looking brighter for the rain;
Around them history swirls like a fog.
You swear you never mean to leave again
For Denmark.
                For here's wine to make you laugh,
And crowds that shout and hurry out of breath
To see the Queen, or a two-headed calf,
And jugglers with a sudden cure for death.

Don't think your sins are a prerogative.
In Paris there is nothing to forgive.

## II

You love, you're loved: she's pretty and she's clever,
A girl with black hair fitting at your throat
Like a violin: it seems she never
Under your fingers gives out one false note.
You talk the smallest matter three times over.
Sure, if you didn't, all the world would love her.

You have her heart, and that's a kind of pledge.
Still, so much sweetness sets your teeth on edge,
And I can see you on the sunny days
Fishing for a siren off the quais.
Your argument: beauty's to be admired
Unless you're blind. What then, and not desired?

## III

"Dear Sir,
          You have been absent from your classes
At the Sorbonne . . ."
                    l'œuvre, l'homme, le milieu
Bray all the cacaphonic little asses.
It all depends upon the point of view.

And then, you've been too credulous in a way,
Read Villon, Ronsard, Du Bellay.
Let them send warnings written in such rhyme
To pick no roses—and you'll not waste time.


## IV

The day was misty, then at once was spring,
She was a dancing girl, no icicle;
No sooner had she set your young heart beating
Than she turned maudlin, cursed and fickle,
And all her tears were running down your face.

You sit like a successful thief, spendthrift,
Letting her jewels trickle through your hands.
You only got what you had eyes to lift,
Her sapphire moon, the stars like diamonds.

This life, if you continue, means disgrace.


## V

A night sky like the passion of a saint,
That clears to let the sudden moon look through.
It seems the very gods come here to paint
And hang their pictures up for public view.

Not like that sullen city in the West
Blazing in a romantic solitude,
Where each American's a self-made artist
Who knows his masterpiece will not be viewed.

# VI

A letter in the morning . . . it's your father.
You hold it to the light . . . probably words
Of good advice, when you had rather
Have his signature to buy new swords.

What's this! It's not your father's hand at all:
The Government . . . eggs must be going bad.
The pages with official seals out-bawl
Their meaning, and you gather

Your father's killed, your sister has gone mad.

# VII

Each man has his Hamlet, that dark other
Self who is the conscience left behind,
Who should be cherished dearly as a brother
But is a sort of madness of the mind:
A serious dark-dressed entire shape
From which no slightest duty can escape.

And every man his Denmark, that dark country,
Familiar, incestuous, to which
He must return, in his turn to stand sentry
Until his blood has filled the Castle ditch,
And clear his father's honor with his life,
And take a perfect ignorance to wife.

To Denmark, then. To face the breaking storm,
The ghosts, the duty, the ingratitude.
God knows you wished that thinking man no harm
And Paris seemed a lasting interlude.
But that the stream of life may be renewed
One man must die, the other may sleep warm.

# Yes Yes

The sun hangs from a crag
Of gray cloud.
The unmarried American Church in Paris
Revolves around the Eiffel Tower
That stands like a startled giraffe.
Thousands of policemen take flight;
The air is full of their black wings
And white beaks.
It is spring and a sound of running
Water in lavabos, cracking
Of celluloid collars.
Fifteen students pass on four bicycles
With red calves and hare-lips
Knapsacks spears and goggles;
They are going fishing underwater.
The sun is reversible and may be used
As a moon when necessary.

The poodles of spring
Are on winter's traces.

# Resistance

On the winding road under the white Alp
A cross and photograph: "Here cowardly slain
Jean Gardère of the Résistance."

The war has been finished three years now
But still your photograph (the best they had)
Makes the enormous sky look like a dark room.

Was it machine-gun or bayonet? In the back?
How did you resist
The actual unimagined agony?

Was it because a German stole your cow,
Because you'd read Rimbaud when you were twelve,
Or were your papers slightly out of order?

Or did you cherish the tricolor, which, in a ribbon,
Decorates your darkening photograph?
That's what the dead are for, to answer questions.

Past your leaning cross the skiers go laughing
To the sun-struck slopes, blue and red and white.
Only a fancy orders those colors aright.

The wind whispers a secret. The wind says
Resisters are somewhat silly. This white
Of fallen snow is the international

Color, which all our lives in a perfect world
Would have, and souls in heaven too.
Your scarlet flow is neither here nor there.

You felt perhaps the gesture to be out-dated
As a boy's dream, a story of knights in armor.
Nevertheless, you made it in slow motion

On the frozen surface of the stony road,
Your feeble flurry of resistance,
That you, not the living, might seem out of place.

# Carentan O Carentan

Trees in the old days used to stand
And shape a shady lane
Where lovers wandered hand in hand
Who came from Carentan.

This was the shining green canal
Where we came two by two
Walking at combat-interval.
Such trees we never knew.

The day was early June, the ground
Was soft and bright with dew.
Far away the guns did sound,
But here the sky was blue.

The sky was blue, but there a smoke
Hung still above the sea
Where the ships together spoke
To towns we could not see.

Could you have seen us through a glass
You would have said a walk
Of farmers out to turn the grass,
Each with his own hay-fork.

The watchers in their leopard suits
Waited till it was time,
And aimed between the belt and boot
And let the barrel climb.

I must lie down at once, there is
A hammer at my knee.
And call it death or cowardice,
Don't count again on me.

Everything's all right, Mother,
Everyone gets the same
At one time or another.
It's all in the game.

I never strolled, nor ever shall,
Down such a leafy lane.
I never drank in a canal,
Nor ever shall again.

There is a whistling in the leaves
And it is not the wind,
The twigs are falling from the knives
That cut men to the ground.

Tell me, Master-Sergeant,
The way to turn and shoot.
But the Sergeant's silent
That taught me how to do it.

O Captain, show us quickly
Our place upon the map.
But the Captain's sickly
And taking a long nap.

Lieutenant, what's my duty,
My place in the platoon?
He too's a sleeping beauty,
Charmed by that strange tune.

Carentan O Carentan
Before we met with you
We never yet had lost a man
Or known what death could do.

# Song: "Rough Winds Do Shake the Darling Buds of May"

Rough winds do shake
                do shake
                        the darling buds of May
The darling buds
           rose-buds
                the winds do shake
That are her breasts,
Those darling buds, dew-tipped, her sighing moods do shake.


She is sixteen
           sixteen
              and her young lust
Is like a thorn
            hard thorn
                among the pink
Of her soft nest.
Upon this thorn she turns, for love's incessant sake.


Her heart will break
              will break
                  unless she may
Let flow her blood
            red blood
                to ease the ache
Where she is pressed.
Then she'll lie still, asleep, who now lies ill, awake.


Well I have seen
           have seen
              one come to joust
Who has a horn
           sweet horn,
                and spear to sink
Before he rests.
When such young buds are torn, the best true loves they make.

# The Arrivistes

[SCENE: *Paris. The moon, small but bright, hovers over the Pont du Carrousel, the untroubled Seine, a few late taxis, the long mass of the Louvre. Two figures saunter along the bank, stopping now and then to wave their arms; bursts of uneasy French and their outlandish attire betray the origin of the flâneurs. The taller one, Athridat, has adopted certain Continental articles of clothing no Frenchman would be seen in, alive or dead. Peter, as always reluctant to do anything out of the ordinary, is dressed so plainly as to give an impression of false pretenses, like an absconding bank clerk, which also attracts curiosity. They enter the scene and are observed, just as Athridat bursts into song:*]

ATHRIDAT

The white moon
Like a baboon
Skips from tree to tree.

The Seine is deep,
The world's asleep,
The cold clock counts three.

PETER

The sky is high,
My throat is dry,
Is there no drink for me?

ATHRIDAT

The white moon
Like a baboon
Skips from tree to tree.

PETER

Must we always make comparisons?

ATHRIDAT

Dear Peter, it's the parallax
That puts us in our place.
Calm seas have sailed us like a Chinese scroll

To this strange city:
Here one is feeding parrots, there another
Performing magic, and the merchants
Converse before their mansions.
The secret is to overhear the world,
Seeing at once all phases of the moon.

### PETER

These syllables of other people's time,
Taken like a tourist, tell no story.

### ATHRIDAT

The secret is to overhear enough
To tell a story.

### PETER

What have we not said about the French?
They limp from war to war
Selling newspapers.
The French bossu
With a stick and basket
Inches over an enormous landscape
Of petites propriétés.
They do not leave the world:
It is torn from them.

### ATHRIDAT

It is the artist's and the soldier's way
To mark how Saint-Germain-des-Prés
Differs from the Great White Way;
How man differs from woman, how
One man from another, then at last
To wander in the tanglewood of wills,
Painting the somber and most native stains
Of evil.

### PETER

Rather, the Roman road.
Be politic, proclaim
No boundaries except barbarians.
All men are citizens . . .

None, none shall die.
The Nations are preparing such a draft
This hour at Chaillot.

ATHRIDAT

Meanwhile, the Cow jumped over the Moon
And the little Dog laughed.
On windy steppes the Russians gnash their teeth . . .

Not in our time, O Peter, nor in theirs
Was Man or Men decided. Once again
I tender the New Testament to you:
Be secret, saintly, and conservative,
Rendering unto Caesar everything
Of metallic content.

PETER

Are you yet preparing that still life
You spoke of once?

ATHRIDAT

The same, although I always start again.

[*Song by Athridat*]

The rails of the Transatlantic Bar
Will never be gold for me.
I have seen Liberty in her car
Like a story once told to me;
The songs are vanished into air
I learned at Mother's knee;
And with a sigh, and with a tear
I've left my own country.

Tonight the unseen servant who
Lurks in the shrubbery
Has placed an orange and a few
Red cherries in the sky.
The stories that they told of you,
My mistress, my Paris,
Will in this magic night come true,
Or never will they be.

Last night a man I'd often met
Came dripping through the rain.
He'd travelled all day, and he'd sat
Up all night in the train.
"At last," he said, "the job is set,
Your Castle in Cockayne,
Room, board and cash, provided that
You never use your brain."

The sword that flatly strikes the air,
As Hebrew psalms complain,
Harries us eastward everywhere.
I shall not turn again,
But go, with just one backward stare
At ruins that remain
Of love, a salty statue there
On the poetic plain.

PETER

The more you see of life, the less impartial
You seem to be.

ATHRIDAT

And what are you concealing?
[*He points to a paper sticking out of Peter's pocket.*]


PETER

A few lines of my own: a nothing
Scribbled on a napkin.

ATHRIDAT

[*Taking it*]

Why, this shows promise!

PETER

No . . . that's the bill. The other side.

ATHRIDAT

I can't quite make out this word.

PETER

An egg-stain.

ATHRIDAT

This line, is it from the Greek?

PETER

Coffee.

ATHRIDAT

Here, you'd better read it, with the textual notes.

PETER

Well, I call it simply Poem.

ATHRIDAT

A good start, a good title. There you let the audience know right away where you stand. Thus you relax the thinking faculty, remove the necessity to make sense, set up around you a fog, and prevent criticism. Now you have as many exits as a clown. To boo or hiss you now would be inhuman as poking a poor habitant of Bellevue. An excellent title: Poem. I like it.

PETER

To proceed; first the circumstance, then the theory. The first stanza, you must know, was written on arrival in the city, the second after a walk in the park, the third . . .

ATHRIDAT

Enough. The Muse is a goddess but also a woman; she does not prefer those who crawl toward her on hands and knees.

PETER

> The witty and unwise are far from home
> On this long siege our youth have held against
> Cities that never fell: Troy, Paris, Rome,
> With a typewriter or a box of paints.

ATHRIDAT

O criminal!

30

PETER

On their high walls the half-gods come and go,
Expert in speech, and war, and lechery.
The adversaries give back blow for blow,
Escaping through the gates by treachery.

The battle now, because of the great host,
The funerals, the swords that clash in rhyme,
Cannot be won, cannot be even lost,
But is the only way of marking time.

How do you like it?

ATHRIDAT

Fair, fair. Shall I recite the lines I dashed off on my cuff while
   listening?

PETER

Pray do.

ATHRIDAT

Fill up the gas-tank with champagne
And throw away the key
And tell the world we're back again
In old pre-war Paris.

The lonely and the gifted come
To ancient cities where
Nature is silent or struck dumb,
And find their voices there.

The fountain's silly trickle or
Some stone perversity
Make people perpendicular,
Rebuild Rome every day.

Here those who once were wild-life are
Part of the tapestry:
The black panther Baudelaire,
The python Valéry.

Welcome this well-kept garden where
A strange necessity

Compels us to admit we're here
Because we wish to be.

PETER

My stomach's still at home.

ATHRIDAT

If I take you to breakfast, will you come?

PETER

And were I to accept, how could you pay?
You borrowed from me only yesterday.

ATHRIDAT

I put it on a horse called The Last Ditch.

PETER

Bravo! He came in first! We've struck it rich! . . .

ATHRIDAT

No, as the matter went he didn't place.

PETER

You've been at poker, then? You had the ace . . .

ATHRIDAT

O no. I swore off gambling, and I sat
In an Auteuil café saying: "That's that!"
Where, all at once, struck up a hue and cry:
"Thief, thief!" A burly type came running by.
Without a second thought I grabbed his knees . . .
A tumble, and a potful of police.
I'd saved somebody's stolen wallet, and . . .

PETER

He thanked you tearfully, and pressed your hand . . .

ATHRIDAT

No, no. You see, they thought I was the thief.
When he confessed, imagine my relief.
Well, as to my hotel I was returning

I passed a building that was fiercely burning:
A woman with her babes trapped on the roof
While in the street the crowd still gaped, aloof.
With tooth and nail I clambered to their aid,
But, when I'd brought them down, the Mayor said:
"Are you a licensed fireman? Let us see
Your card (and quickly) of identity!"

PETER

But surely, from the husband some reward?

ATHRIDAT

I think he set his house off, feeling bored.
Well, all around I got such dirty looks
I'm lucky that my name's not on the books.

PETER

But, Athridat, I thought I heard you say
You'd take me in to breakfast, and you'd pay?

ATHRIDAT

After such narrow shaves, clear signs of grace,
I have a happy feeling of great space.
I'd treat the city, if I had the mean.

PETER

It doesn't rustle, and it isn't green.
I'll pay as usual!
But wait: here comes a wolf, a bat, a shark,
A character that operates by dark!

[Enter Black-Marketeer]

BLACK-MARKETEER

Anything American to sell, gentlemen?

ATHRIDAT

How much?

33

## BLACK-MARKETEER

Trois cents soixante the traveller's check: trois cents quatre-
vingt . . .

## PETER

Scram, you gangster. It's people like you who cause financial
instability.

[*Exit Black-Marketeer*]

## ATHRIDAT

The cheap crook! When everybody's offering four hundred
on the dollar!

[*Re-enter Black-Marketeer, disguised with a
drooping moustache*]

## BLACK MARKETEER

You wish nice cabaret, gentlemen? Tzigane orchestra, or
maybe little burlesques style 1900. Maybe something
more particular: specialties of Paris?

## PETER AND ATHRIDAT

No.

[*Exit Black-Marketeer*]

## ATHRIDAT

The hunger in my vitals
Is for some credible extravaganza
Such as Stendhal suggests:
A woman in a window and
A battlefield with mountains bright beyond.

## PETER

Remember, in la Musée de l'Armée
A cuirasse, souvenir of Waterloo . . .

## ATHRIDAT

A cannon ball had torn through front and back;
The metal still remained malevolent.

34

PETER

The horrid orifice, I thought, would groan.

[*A groan is heard, and they recoil*]

PETER

Some spirit moves
Under the bridge. The moonlight on the roofs,
These shadowed avenues and statues gaunt,
Provide an invitation to the haunt.
The hour is advanced: I fear, my friend,
That supernatural prodigies portend!

ATHRIDAT

Stand fast, Peter. If it sound again
I'll challenge it to answer, man to man.

[*A second groan, and a sound of horse's hooves,
a faint huzza as of charging cavalry, a
commingled booming, a flash in the air and
horrid gulp and thud. A white powdery
light plays over the bridge, on which a fig-
ure, certainly not of this world, material-
izes. Peter and Athridat regard it,
petrified.*]

GHOST

From regions infernal,
        Turning and twisting
I rise at the summons
        Of those now existing.

PETER

[*Aside to Athridat*]

I didn't ask him to turn up; did you?

GHOST

A word from your lip
        Can sting like a whip.
How hellish these regions
        Of worldly opinions!

35

[*The apparition appears in cavalry uniform.
On its body the broken cuirass is brassily
represented.*]

GHOST

We are the tongues that hang
        At authors' sleepless ears,
Until the Sturm und Drang
        In folio appears.

ATHRIDAT

Alas, poor ghost! You mean to be published!

GHOST

If I can win your sympathy,
        Already far extended,
To recreate reality,
        My tortures may be ended.

[*The Ghost lifts an arm. The darkness is rolled
back like a curtain, so presenting a small
stage upon which scenery of trees, hills, riv-
ers is being moved and several spectral fig-
ures are bustling about.*]

GHOST

The leavetaking!

[*Before the eyes of Peter and Athridat rises a
small village on the River Yonne, of the
year 1815. A hussar, original of our Ghost,
is seen embracing and being embraced by his
family. The Mayor is there, very busy and
pompous. Also: the parish priest, the sol-
dier's white-haired mother, his grizzled fa-
ther, a blushing maid. The Mayor mounts
the platform and in a dumb show speaks at
length. A trumpet down the street an-
nounces the arrival of a regiment; before its
invigorating notes urchins scamper happily.
The Ghost swings on to his horse, which
rears and snorts; the villagers cheer; his fa-*]

*ther hands the hussar his sword; tears are*
*shed, and the regiment moves out toward*
*its marshalling area.*]

CHORUS OF VILLAGERS

To win the heart of woman
Is every hero's aim,
So, when the drums are drumming
And all the bullets humming,
To horse! You're only human,
    And it's a hero game
To win the heart of woman.

And would you live forever
When all the bugles blow?
Leave thinking to the clever,
Your melancholy fever . . .
To horse! It's now or never:
    You're packed off, and you go.

THE HUSSARS

When all the bugles blow!

THE VILLAGERS

And would you live forever?

Don't worry, we'll remember
The sacrifice you've made.
The hundreds you dismember,
Your cold camps in December,
Shall keep our old tongues limber
    Whenever music's played . . .
Don't worry, we'll remember.

THE HUSSARS

To win the heart of woman
Is every hero's aim . . .

GHOST                    [*As the Scene fades*]

The trade of woman is love
And man's is war. Were these removed,
Life would be simply indescribable.
Utopia
Is the illuminated nightmare
From which we wake in horror
To embrace the stinking form beside us
Of lover or corpse.

PETER

This spirit is in hell.

GHOST

When princes did great wrongs
I was present.

ATHRIDAT

Why, so were we all!

GHOST

And all shall burn. But silence!
The scene . . .

> [*The stage is used again by forms and shapes
> which illustrate the high-pitched aerial rec-
> itative which follows. Whether or not these
> words are actually uttered is not certain;
> in their confused state Peter and Athridat
> cannot separate words from meaning.*]

## "Waterloo"

[*Recitative*]

Uncounted scattered fires had not brightened
The drizzle on the eve of Waterloo.
The Ardennes were uneasy, and it lightened
Still over Ligny. A far trumpet blew
One falling note that thrilled the sentry through
Upon his lonely round. The hoarfrost whitened
The bayonet, the sleeper's twisted shoe.

Beside him on his circle went a shade
In Roman helmet, with a hollow face.
Since Caesar's time how many marches made
To bring the eagles back to the same place!
A change in uniform, the cut of lace,
But what the Emperor or Caesar said
Had the same end: the Legion's changeless pace.

And morning called the armies, and they came,
But hesitantly with the hawks ahead.
The scouts first beat the cover for the game,
While conscripts gazed at prisoners in red,
And ducked from shots that arched high overhead:
A trickle to the rear of halt and lame,
Their faces chalky, clasping where they bled.

His regiment champed on its metal, for
Their field was viewless, and no enemy.
The only indication of the war
Was when a spent projectile hit a tree;
And now and then one man or two or three
Ran over the horizon, or a score
Of generals came gaily prancing by.

As patience failed, a pretty braided boy
Rode up, saluted, shouted something loud.
The Colonel waved his saber: cheers of joy
Ran through the ranks. The horses raised their bowed
Ruminating heads, and in a crowd
The regiment went off: a shining toy
Seen from the height of that one watching cloud.

As they rode on, the rhythmic hoofbeats mixed
Into a music passionate and clear.
Each man bolt upright in his saddle fixed,
With armor plate, and greaves, and skin of bear:
They left three blackened cannon to the rear . . .
The gunners, at their smoky trade asphyxt,
Stood up and shook their ramrods with a cheer.

The crest at last! Before them stretched a brown
And littered slope. Horses in full career
Were dashing without riders; some were down,

39

Bellowing with wide nostrils. Then the air
In ripples split with an intenser glare
Before a long dark line that broke the crown
Of Mont St. Jean, the shattered Scottish square.

Now gathering great impetus, the mass
Of horses, men and lances never broke
Formation, but presented one cuirass
Of steel continuous, curled round with smoke.
And then the cannon of the English spoke.
Great holes appeared, through which a ship might pass:
And at that voice the single man awoke.

The wounded sank below: above, the sky
Arched quivering through veils of shifting red;
The sun stared like the pupil of an eye.
He felt the wind, and heard the whistling lead,
The screaming of the stallion, the tread . . .
And now, as a spectator, one long cry
Wrenched from his body, riding still, though dead.

> [*The Scene fades; the Ghost ceases his gesticu-
> lations; Athridat and Peter shake off their
> bemusement, and . . .*]

ATHRIDAT

The story of your death, this spectacle,
Was like an inhalation of fresh air.
But of what purpose to us living
In prison still? Romantic Ghost,
Be practical!

GHOST

Look East.

PETER

The horizon trembles, grumbles, the skyline
Flashes and flickers. It is
The hour of betrayal,
Of amputation of right hands,
The time when tongues
Are torn by the root.

ATHRIDAT

There by the white road winding
Comes the clank clank clank
Of the Legion, each man carrying
Kitchen equipment, buckler, spear
And at his thigh the short sword
Like a part of himself. Tall plumes
Nodding warward, twenty miles a day.
What road, peasant?
                    What month . . .

PETER

Those who administer military justice

GHOST

Shall leave no ruins
But what a horse can canter without stumbling.

> [*The white light fades. The Ghost holds up his right hand in a gesture of farewell.*]

GHOST

Your turn on guard!

> [*A cock crows. The Ghost starts, and is dislimned; the scene fades and curls away in a light vapor blown over the parapets of the bridge, and . . .*]

ATHRIDAT

Sauve qui peut!

PETER

Collect yourself. Observe,
It's nearly day. This European scene
Is like a comedy, each age an act
In one old plot the public know
By heart. All that matters is the style.
You are American. Is it worthwhile
Getting excited?

## ATHRIDAT

You call me to my senses. The exhilaration
Of other people's imagination
It was betrayed me.
These actors are realities
In an echoing world. We, on the other side,
Are still intruders to our atmosphere.
Concrete and cactus are the real
American tragedy.
We should collect our souvenirs and leave.

## PETER

Little by little
Light recovers the city, ruined
No less by Monet than David.
The earth, so often saturated
By colors false as blood, takes on
Your American gray.

## ATHRIDAT

The West was never an original,
But one of many copies.

## PETER

The sun is up. The shouting dies away.

## ATHRIDAT

The Seine winds like white wine across the table
Between the candelabra and a vegetable.
Looking upriver, I observe
Water's polished slate, the hazy sun
And trees in shadowed blocks
With green or yellow brackets:
A quiet mezzotint, not yet the glitter
Of each leaf in the afternoon.

The roofs are undetailed, flat domes,
Oblongs. The sky's a powdery cone
Whose mist as it's absorbed, not blown,
Turns purple at the base, above

The lightest blue. A fisher promenades,
One hand in pocket, with a big black dog.

The barge Espoir
Thumps upstream with wet laundry
On her gay lines.
Lend me your camera.

# Good News of Death and Other Poems
## 1955

# The True Weather for Women

Young women in their April moodiness
Complain of showers, for they cannot go
Swimming, or to the courts to play tennis.
But if they suffer from a gentle blow,
What will the storm, the terror of saints, do?
If April presses their green tenderness
How will they stand the full weight of the snow?

Now they are killing time, with darts and chess,
And others dancing to the radio,
And some for kisses take a turn to guess
At names, and laugh at tales of love also.
Jenny, in her hot tub, repaints a toe,
Admiring her perfect nakedness
While thunders crack and summer lightnings glow.

There is one date that they will keep, although
They have been often late to come to men,
For death hits all such deer with his long bow
And drags them by the neck into his den,
And there eternally they may complain
And tap and gesture in a frantic show
And look at summer through a windowpane.

Wind up the pulse with poppy, sleep them so!
Their selfishness will always entertain,
And even death will seem small weather woe
When love is all their sun and all their rain.
The clock will never strike, adjusted then
To their sweet drowsings, and they will not know
How punctual death is, or else how slow.

47

# As Birds Are Fitted
## to the Boughs

As birds are fitted to the boughs
That blossom on the tree
And whisper when the south wind blows—
So was my love to me.

And still she blossoms in my mind
And whispers softly, though
The clouds are fitted to the wind,
The wind is to the snow.

# A Woman Too Well Remembered

Having put on new fashions, she demands
New friends. She trades her beauty and her humor
In anybody's eyes. If diamonds
Were dark, they'd sparkle so. Her aura is
The glance of scandal and the speed of rumor.

One day, as I recall, when we conversed
In kisses, it amused her to transmit
"What hath God wrought!"—the message that was first
Sent under the Atlantic. Nonsense, yet
It pleases me sometimes to think of it.

*Noli me tangere* was not her sign.
Her pilgrim trembled with the softest awe.
She was the only daughter of a line
That sleeps in poetry and silences.
She might have sat upon the Sphinx's paw.

Then is she simply false, and falsely fair?
(The promise she would break she never made)
I cannot say, but truly can compare,
For when the stars move like a steady fire
I think of her, and other faces fade.

# The Man Who Married Magdalene

The man who married Magdalene
Had not forgiven her.
God might pardon every sin . . .
Love is no pardoner.

Her hands were hollow, pale, and blue,
Her mouth like watered wine.
He watched to see if she were true
And waited for a sign.

It was old harlotry, he guessed,
That drained her strength away,
So gladly for the dark she dressed,
So sadly for the day.

Their quarrels made her dull and weak
And soon a man might fit
A penny in the hollow cheek
And never notice it.

At last, as they exhausted slept,
Death granted the divorce,
And nakedly the woman leapt
Upon that narrow horse.

But when he woke and woke alone
He wept and would deny
The loose behavior of the bone
And the immodest thigh.

# The Window

These are the houses of the poor—
Strange animals . . . they live in view. . . .
That woman, on the second floor,
There's nothing that she wants to do.

She sits unmoving in the light,
She combs her hair, walks to and fro,
Argues with someone out of sight . . .
There's nowhere that she wants to go.

She cleans and cooks, sits down to eat,
And does the dishes. When she dies
The neighbors wash her dirty feet
And draw the blinds that were her eyes.

# Memories of a Lost War

The guns know what is what, but underneath
In fearful file
We go around burst boots and packs and teeth
That seem to smile.

The scene jags like a strip of celluloid,
A mortar fires,
Cinzano falls, Michelin is destroyed,
The man of tires.

As darkness drifts like fog in from the sea
Somebody says
"We're digging in." Look well, for this may be
The last of days.

Hot lightnings stitch the blind eye of the moon,
The thunder's blunt.
We sleep. Our dreams pass in a faint platoon
Toward the front.

Sleep well, for you are young. Each tree and bush
Drips with sweet dew,
And earlier than morning June's cool hush
Will waken you.

The riflemen will wake and hold their breath.
Though they may bleed
They will be proud a while of something death
Still seems to need.

# The Battle

Helmet and rifle, pack and overcoat
Marched through a forest. Somewhere up ahead
Guns thudded. Like the circle of a throat
The night on every side was turning red.

They halted and they dug. They sank like moles
Into the clammy earth between the trees.
And soon the sentries, standing in their holes,
Felt the first snow. Their feet began to freeze.

At dawn the first shell landed with a crack.
Then shells and bullets swept the icy woods.
This lasted many days. The snow was black.
The corpses stiffened in their scarlet hoods.

Most clearly of that battle I remember
The tiredness in eyes, how hands looked thin
Around a cigarette, and the bright ember
Would pulse with all the life there was within.

# The Heroes

I dreamed of war-heroes, of wounded war-heroes
With just enough of their charms shot away
To make them more handsome. The women moved nearer
To touch their brave wounds and their hair streaked with gray.

I saw them in long ranks ascending the gang-planks;
The girls with the doughnuts were cheerful and gay.
They minded their manners and muttered their thanks;
The Chaplain advised them to watch and to pray.

They shipped these rapscallions, these sea-sick battalions
To a patriotic and picturesque spot;
They gave them new bibles and marksmen's medallions,
Compasses, maps, and committed the lot.

A fine dust has settled on all that scrap metal.
The heroes were packaged and sent home in parts
To pluck at a poppy and sew on a petal
And count the long night by the stroke of their hearts.

# The Ash and the Oak

When men discovered freedom first
The fighting was on foot,
They were encouraged by their thirst
And promises of loot,
And when it feathered and bows boomed
Their virtue was a root.

O the ash and the oak and the willow tree
And green grows the grass on the infantry!

At Malplaquet and Waterloo
They were polite and proud,
They primed their guns with billets-doux
And, as they fired, bowed.
At Appomattox too, it seems
Some things were understood.

O the ash and the oak and the willow tree
And green grows the grass on the infantry!

But at Verdun and at Bastogne
There was a great recoil,
The blood was bitter to the bone
The trigger to the soul,
And death was nothing if not dull,
A hero was a fool.

O the ash and the oak and the willow tree
And that's an end of the infantry!

# American Preludes

## I

This isle hath many goodly woods and deer,
Conies and fowl in incredible abundance;
The woods, not such as you find in Bohemia,
Barren and fruitless, but the highest cedars,
Better than those of Libanus, and pines,
Cypress and sassifras and lentisk:
To them the sea winds owe their wafting spice.

Discharging our muskets
A flock of cranes, most white, arose by us
With such a cry as if an army of men
Had shouted together.

We saw not any of the people
Until, the third day,
In a little boat
Three of them appeared, and one of them
Went on shore, to whom we rowed.
He attended
Without any sign of fear.

When he had spoken,
Though we understood not a word,
Of his own accord he came boldly aboard us.
We gave him a shirt,
A hat, wine and meat, which he liked well.

The next day
Came divers boats, and in one of them
The King's brother.
His name was Granganameo,
The King is called Wingina,
The country, Wingandacao.

The women wear their hair long on both sides,
The men on one; they are of color yellow;
Their hair is black, yet we saw children
That had very fair chestnut colored hair.

For an armor he would have engaged us
A bag of pearl, but we refused,
As not regarding it, that we might the better
Learn where it grew.

This discovery was so welcome into England
That it pleased her Majesty
To call this country Virginia.

## II

A flag-blue day with scarlets of furled cloud
A fowler's morning in the water reeds
Here on a white horse comes the General
Shaking the green tatters with his drums
And tanagers out of the cherry trees.

A farmer's view cut up in cherry pies
The fowler packs tobacco in his pipe
The branches are pricked out in violet
The farmer turns the plough and jackdaws hop
The General tugs at his wooden teeth.

The new farm will not bear too much Satan
A sudden child peers out from cherry trees
At rumps and trumpets and the General
Going with a tight rein and aching jaw
To carve the Lion, crack the Lobster's claw.

## III

The white walls
Undulate with sea shadows. In the fields
The cypresses stand up like somber flames,
And yellow roses tangle from the walls.

Vaquero, I have seen your ending days,
Looped in a lariat, dragged at the heels
Of the black horses.

Under the eucalyptus tree
There is the girl who waits for me,
Her brown feet stretched to the salt tongues of sea.

57

Cathedral, vessel of God, wait for me,
Where potsherds and faded roses
Are cast beside the wall, and cypresses
Weep, sad sisters.

Cathedral, vessel of the dead,
O cast off these white anchors, Miserere,
And spread your spinnakers Magnificat
Laudemus to the horizon!

Blessings perch there like birds,
Saints gather like gulls
For pecks of bread.
The bow is booming in the blood of Christ.

But she does not weep, she does not chant Miserere,
Her eyes are green as the shallow sea,
The one who is waiting for me.


IV

Hudson, come down from your leaf-stroked cascades,
Angry so soon to be encased in ice,
Gone is the Sleeping Man and gone
The steamboat floating upstream like a swan,
But the calm sleep that raised these Palisades
To new, majestic augurs still persuades.

Green in summer; winter, white and cold;
The softest season neither young nor old,
Which two red Indians bring in,
Pocahontas in her painted skin.

The last Elizabethans reappear,
Court orange and fool's yellow. The bright air
Rasps the hunter's lungs; he walks peak-capped,
Flanneled, rubbered, wrapped,
His pockets bulging with fat shotgun shells.

Maple and berry dogwood, oak, are kings.
The axe is lively and your pale palm stings
While Echo claps her hands on the bare hill.
The scene is clear. The air is chill.

# West

On US 101
I felt the traffic running like a beast,
Roaring in space.

                    Tamalpais
The red princess slopes
In honeyed burial from hair to feet;
The sharp lifting fog
Uncurtains Richmond and the ridge
—With two red rubies set upon the bridge—
And curtains them again.

Ranching in Bolinas, that's the life,
If you call cattle life.
To sit on a veranda with a glass
And see the sprinklers watering your land
And hear the peaches dropping from the trees
And hear the ocean in the redwood trees,

The whales of time,
Masts of the long voyages of earth,
In whose tall branches day
Hangs like a Christmas toy.

On their red columns drowse
The eagles battered at the Western gate;
These trees have held the eagles in their state
When Rome was still a rumor in the boughs.

# Early in the Morning

Early in the morning
The dark Queen said,
"The trumpets are warning
There's trouble ahead."
Spent with carousing,
With wine-soaked wits,
Antony drowsing
Whispered, "It's
Too cold a morning
To get out of bed."

The army's retreating,
The fleet has fled,
Caesar is beating
His drums through the dead.
"Antony, horses!
We'll get away,
Gather our forces
For another day . . ."
"It's a cold morning,"
Antony said.

Caesar Augustus
Cleared his phlegm.
"Corpses disgust us.
Cover them."
Caesar Augustus
In his time lay
Dying, and just as
Cold as they,
On the cold morning
Of a cold day.

# Aegean

Where only flowers fret
And some small passionate
Bird sings, the trumpets sounded yesterday.
The famous ships are gone,
Troy fades, and the face that shone—
Fair Helen, in her tower—could not stay.

Where are the temples set
Their gods would not forget,
The trophies, and the altars? Echo, say.
There's no one any more
But Echo on the shore,
And Echo only laughs and runs away.

Though still the olive glows
Like silver, and the rose
Is glittering and fresh, as in their day,
No witnesses remain
Of battles on the plain
And the bright oar and the oar spray.

# Mississippi

When we went down the river on a raft
So smooth it was and easy it would seem
Land moved but never we. Clouds faded aft
In castles. Trees would hurry in the dream
Of water, where we gazed, with this log craft
America suspended on a gleam.

The days were mostly pipes and fishing lines,
Though for a turn or two we had a king,
A Nonesuch with his royal monkeyshines,
But treacherous, for all his capering.
The naked wickedness of his designs
Brought on Democracy, a steady thing.

Steady but alarming. Rip-tooth snags
Are wrapped in smoothness like the tiger's hide,
And when she blows, chickens and carpet bags
Go roiling seaward on the yellow tide.
And Brady photographs the men like flags
Still tilted in the charges where they died.

The river is too strong for bank or bar,
The landmarks change, and nothing would remain
But for the man who travels by a star,
Whose careful eye adjusts the course again . . .
Still shadow at the wheel, his rich cigar
Glowed like a point of rectitude—Mark Twain.

If ever there were Mississippi nights,
If ever there was Dixie, as they sing,
Cry, you may cry, for all your true delights
Lost with the banjo and the Chicken Wing
Where old St. Joe slid on the water lights
And on into the dark, diminishing.

# Islanders

## I

Poetry has no place, still you must choose
A starting point—say, with the displaced Jews
Who come to this small park from the ends of earth:
They weep with sorrow and expect a birth,
Their gutturals disrupt the summer nights
While darkness slowly laps the river lights.
Their skins are wrinkled like fine handkerchiefs
Of Brussels, intricately stitched with griefs.
The wind that stirs their soft curls makes you cold
Thinking of Belsen and of Buchenwald.
Their tears obscure your Christ like candlegrease—
A swinging acrobat, no Prince of Peace!
Cry thief! Someone has stolen the true Cross!
Go to these Jews, accuse them of your loss!

Poetry has no place, but life is kind.
Revenge yourself on a girl—she will not mind.
A glossy, sulky one comes strolling by;
The loiterers compete to catch her eye,
But, even as you stare, she's whisked away
By a sport jacket and a new coupé.
Tonight when he brings her home—"Oi, from his place!"
Her father cries, her mother slaps her face,
She packs her bag while the children wail and shout,
Her father asks her where she's going—"Out!"
And that means America. She may go far
And hang over California like a star,
Returning with affection fierce as spite
To lavish wealth and set the old rooms right.

This tapeworm, poetry, won't make you fat:
It's time for supper at the automat.
Those faces are reflections of your own,
Faces that cannot bear to be alone,
Faces at whose back scream nightingales,
Faces that cannot endure the sound of bells . . .
Could they exchange their hopes—no, they will stare
Into their own, out in the dark somewhere,

Gulping their beans. Each at some point preferred
To live like this rather than say a word—
Was it "I love you" or another "Yes" . . .
Each is fascinated with some strange success.
Their lips move silently; they are living again
Some secret hour of familiar pain.

## II

In streets that darken, sinister for miles,
You think of Egypt and the crocodiles.
These massive blocks, from which the sun has fled,
Remind you of the labors of the dead—
Dull pyramids, too large to be destroyed,
That, even ruined, could not be enjoyed.
The slaves are not devoted to their toil—
They gather sullenly, at dark recoil
As though from gods of which they are ashamed,
Propitiated, served, but never named.

I see you suddenly transfixed and caught
In traffic—pale and spectral as a thought.
They drive on curves of steel and swoops of stone
So fast their similes will find them gone.
They will not wait for you—they are not flowers
Or statues, but the masks of worldly powers.
Like stars at speed they dream in a bright coil,
Their brains are glitterings, their blood is oil,
They have no past, they call their souls their own . . .
But time eludes them, time, and time alone.
They're in a tearing hurry, to enrich
The undertaker and to spoil a ditch.

## III

I see you standing in the square called Times.
The lights spell out Adventure, Passion, Crimes,
Dances of Bali, Hitler's Loves, The Whip,
And sometimes Shakespeare for your scholarship—
Immediate seating, smoking in the rear . . .
The moon is blazing like a sign for beer.

To those who have been nourished on the swarm
This is a hayride, harvest on the farm.
Here come the handsome—and the rich, the smart
Arrive in Cadillacs that shake the heart—
The thief, the pimp, the actress and the whore . . .
Arabia, to the astonished poor.

The blind man counts the nickels in his cup,
But eyes go flying sideways, flying up
Like dazzled birds. Beyond the daily wage
They're caught in their own lives, the outer cage,
And cry for exits, hoping to be shown
A way by others, who have lost their own.

And yet, seen from a distance and a height,
How haunting are the islands of the night,
The shores on which we dream, with the deep tide
Of darkness rushing in on every side.


## IV

And you, an islander—listen! There it moves!
The sea reminds us of our early loves.
This is a liner of stone, with star-cleaving funnels,
These streets are the decks, we crowd to the blazing gunwales.
Look up at the men who paint a precarious mast—
The scaffolds are tossed by the wind, they hold carelessly fast,
They walk in the clouds, they gaze into blue gulfs of ether . . .

If you too stood in the storm, exposed to the weather,
In the pulse of sound and silence, wafting westward you might see
Another Aphrodite tiptoe on the white-curled sea.
If you could cast the moorings of the bridges and set sail,
Feel the waves of time go under, clinging to the sea-wet rail,
To meet her as she comes again, as once to Cyprus' bay,
And she wrings her golden hair out, that is striped and streaked
      with gray,
On the horses, the blue horses, that stand still on foaming feet—
The goddess of the ocean, with gray eyes and wrinkled knees,
Who breaks the generations to make more men's pelvises . . .
The city tilts and founders in a turbulence of gulls,
The waves regurgitate their fish, torn nets and splintered hulls,

And with one wind all will be drowned, to be God's bellyful,
Until with shining weeds enwound they rise more beautiful.

You find yourself at the Circle. This is no masted ship!
Those towers are the stalagmites of stars that slowly drip—
Flowers freaked with blue and white on stalks that seem to twist
To some great height where love is made and birds sing in a mist—
One rose, pistilla of light with red cloud petals,
Rose of the heart hammered thin, of the most precious metals—
A chisel driven aslant, a silicate wedge . . .

Enough of these images—they set the teeth on edge!
Life, if you like, is a metaphor of death—
The difference is you, a place for the passing of breath.
That is what man is. He is the time between,
The palpable glass through which all things are seen.
Nothing. Silence. A syllable. A word.
Everything.

        After your death this poem occurred.
You were the honored fragments from the Greek.
After your death these stones would move and speak.

# Good News of Death

## A Pastoral

THE PERSONS:
CHLOE, *a shepherdess, wife of* PETER
CUDDY, *a businessman*
PETER, *a shepherd*
ROLAND (*also called* ORESTES), *a sheep*
*First Fury*
*Second Fury*
*Third Fury*
*A shepherd*

[*The place is mountainous, the weather turning cold; in the last scene night falls and a star is rising.*]

### SCENE ONE

CHLOE: Stop and tell us, Mister Cuddy, where at such a pace you're going.

CUDDY: I never stop for nobody unless there's money owing.

CHLOE: Won't you tell us, Mister Cuddy, what it is that's on your mind. . . .
Is it too much work and study, or is Phyllis still unkind?

CUDDY: Good day, shepherds, live at leisure, but we other businessmen
In hard work must take our pleasure, in our cow and pig and hen.

PETER: Is Amaryllis on your mind, that makes you run so fast?

CUDDY: No, Amaryllis is unkind, I have no time to waste.

PETER: There must be cause for such a haste. Say, is your Holstein lost?
Or news of war with Russia? Cuddy, have you seen a ghost?

CUDDY: The marketplace is waiting. Give me room to stretch my legs.
While I stand here hesitating, up goes butter, down go eggs.

CHLOE:      Won't you stop if Chloe asks it, just a while to rest your
              knees?
              See here, Cuddy, in my basket I have wine and sausages.
CUDDY:      I do not trust a lady that is naked as she is.
              I may be late already. I must run. Excuse me please.

                                    [*Exit* CUDDY, *running*]


## SCENE TWO

CHLOE:      As I was saying, you can't even keep
              Your wife in clothes, yet here's another sheep.
              You always buy what other people sell.
              My mother used to warn me . . .
PETER:                                          Stop that bell!
CHLOE:      I'll ring it as I please. Does all this prove
              Your promises, your pledge of "richer love"?
              Now you take Phoebe, who just married Ted . . .
PETER:      Who hasn't taken her?
CHLOE:                                What's that you said?
              *Her* husband doesn't dress her in a leaf.
              If you were more like Colin . . .
PETER:                                          And a thief.
CHLOE:      I think the time is not too far away
              That I'll sprout horns, bear wool, and answer *Baa!*
              Oh, why did I become a shepherd's wife!
PETER:      The fairest woman chose to share that life,
              And for the passion of a shepherd boy
              The very gods fought on the plains of Troy.

              Between Scamander and the sky-blue sea
              A city stood, that held the golden key
              To Hellespont. Close by, on Ida's steep
              King Priam's son, young Paris, kept his sheep.
              To him, one sunny afternoon, there came
              Three naked goddesses who knew his name.
              When he'd come to his senses, they said this:
              At the nuptials of Peleus and Thetis
              The gossip goddess, Eris, was excluded.
              She, spiteful as a woman, sulked and brooded,
              And hit on this revenge, to throw an apple

Among them, marked "For the most beautiful."
Three goddesses had claimed it: here they were,
Juno, Aphrodite, Athena.
And now they asked, it was a small request,
Which did he think in honesty the fairest?
They offered presents. Paris would not budge
(More happy to deliberate than judge).
But Aphrodite, reading in his mind,
Or seeing him already so inclined,
Offered the fairest woman for his own.
She had the apple, and the harm was done.

Now Sparta's king, unlucky Menelaus,
Had brought a young wife, Helen, to his house,
As you or I might put a burning torch
To bed and chamber, parlor, roof, and porch.
Above her patient distaff, the young bride
Would often dream, and as she dreamed she sighed.
Then Paris came. She looked and looked again
And saw the meaning of her dreams made plain.
Without much conversation, they soon crept
Into each other's arms, while statues wept.

At last they ran away, nor heard behind
Trumpets, and towers falling in the wind.
The sail was spread, the sun on the blue sea
Clasped in a net their white intricacy.
He was the spear and she the flopping fish,
He had his Helen, and she had her wish.

How Menelaus' brother, Agamemnon,
Besieged tall Troy until the war was won;
Of Iphigenia and the calm at Aulis,
And of the famous anger of Achilles;
How Clytemnestra, Agamemnon's wife,
Murdered her husband with an altar knife,
And with Orestes ended Pelops' curse,
Are told in epic and dramatic verse.

CHLOE:   So Helen was a kind of shepherdess!
This is a long way from a ragged dress.
Let Phoebe keep her silly goosedown bed!
Just wait until I tell her what you've said!

[ROLAND, *the sheep, comes to the front and, with strange expressions, he speaks*]

ROLAND:    The secret's out. Your story breaks the spell.
My name is not Roland. My name is . . . well,
Call me Orestes.

PETER:                No, impossible!

ROLAND:    When Agamemnon, with his brave allies
Pursuing Paris, was becalmed at Aulis,
Old Calchas, the soothsayer, then advised
The King's own daughter must be sacrificed.
Proud Agamemnon gave her to be killed.
Iphigenia, how the sails were filled!

Ten years they fought at Troy, a cold exile.
But Clytemnestra, the King's wife, meanwhile
Thought of a daughter, by a husband dead,
And first harmed Agamemnon in his bed.
Aegisthus was her lover, soft and sly,
With whom she turned the palace to a sty.

The torches leap, the conqueror returns,
They kill the ox, pour out the holy urns,
He climbs the purple carpet to his wife,
Who smiling whets the sacrificial knife.
They lift the battered helmet, the bronze plates
That Hector dented, and his hot tub waits.

What shout was that? Once more, and yet again!
In his unholy pride my father's slain.

Now Clytemnestra with defiant mien
Rules with Aegisthus, a tyrannic queen;
But Fate, incessant Fate, is at the door
And shakes the roof and undermines the floor.
Electra, my own sister, sullen wench,
Is married to a swineherd, in his stench
To lose her memories. But there's a son,
Orestes, and his whereabouts unknown.
And so I come to Argos, well disguised,
I meet Electra and am recognized.
The stage is set. Aegisthus dies the first,
His pampered fingers clasp the dagger's thrust.
My mother's next. But Nature shudders Stop!

My trembling hands would let the dagger drop,
But the quick god, Apollo (whose strange ways
I have not understood these many days)
Urges revenge. Now Clytemnestra falls
And Matricide goes shrieking through the halls.

A crowd approaches, and with sticks and stones
Would end the curse of Pelops' house at once.
Apollo intervenes. They see, perplexed,
A god against the law.

               The Furies, vexed,
From Hades in their endless coils arise,
I see them at the corners of my eyes,
I run into the dark. . . . And from this day
I run, I run, and can no longer stay
Than sleep, but that's another kind of pain,
And when I sleep I cry to wake again.

But since I've had some practice at disguise,
Sometimes I manage to elude the Furies:
At Delphi for a while as a shoemaker,
In Athens as a critic and a baker.
The god, Apollo, would protect me still,
But he became more unpredictable
Until he vanished out of sight and mind.
Apollo went, and left me here behind.
The Furies followed still; *they* had not changed.
Through more disguises I more madly ranged.
The noble masks the gods once lent to man
Were gone. The age of animals began.
This wool, these horns, are all that stand between
Myself and sights too horrid to be seen.
The poor disguise conceals, until I hear
My name. Then truth compels me to declare
I am Orestes.

                       [*Enter* THE FURIES]


1ST FURY: Where is he, sister?

2ND FURY: Never too far away.

3RD FURY: I hear him, I smell him, Orestes,
          Clytemnestra's bloody boy.

1ST FURY:  Our darling, to the verge of death.

2ND FURY:  Apollo is dead, he cannot help him now.

3RD FURY:  Oho, a pretty ram!

CHLOE:  Peter, I think that I am going to faint.

ROLAND:  Ah, my god, my god,
I see them, they exist, out of my mind or in it.
I am not mad, though there were times I've wished
I might be so. I've gone
Beyond such selfish terror. Come, dull Death,
And may the kind and courteous world
Hear no more of me. Oh, Apollo!

1ST FURY:  Apollo is dead, they've buried Apollo,
And soon you will wish that you might follow.

CHLOE:  Oh, Peter, help me away, I can't stand more.

PETER:  This is more mutton than I bargained for.


## SCENE THREE

[ROLAND *is lying in the foreground. Enter* PETER, *cautiously, and* A
SHEPHERD. *They are armed with sticks.*]

PETER:  I tell you that I saw them. There were three . . .

SHEPHERD:  I've seen that kind myself, especially
When I have had a drink, or even two.

PETER:  This is no joke. And Chloe saw them too.

SHEPHERD:  Why, here he is, your consecrated sheep . . .
Roland!

PETER:  Orestes!

SHEPHERD:  This is a strange sleep.

PETER:  No, feel his pulse. He's dead. He'll never more
Nibble the salty sedges at the shore,
Nor juicy hill grass. He has filled his crop,
No more will chew, and ruminate, and drop.
Bleat, bleat, you lambs, it will be of no use,
And bawl for Roland now, you widowed ewes,
For all your bellies, swollen not with wind,
Must yield more orphans to call Fate unkind.

Well, all is over. Nothing's left to do
But bear him to some archipelago
That's high above the storm. There he will have
A simple shaft to mark his tragic grave.

[*Exeunt in a dead march, bearing* ROLAND]


SCENE FOUR

[PETER, CHLOE, THE SHEPHERD. *Enter* CUDDY, *running.*]

CHLOE :    Won't you stop and tell us, Cuddy, where at such a pace
you're going.

PETER:    He never stops for nobody unless there's money owing.

CUDDY:    I am following the rumor that is out and running wild.
They say that Christ has come about like any other child.
The murderer, the usurer, the robber, and all such,
Except the men of Caesar, are forgiven by his touch.
The hanged man, the stabbed man, the man who's
crucified,
The man who drank and drabbed too much and sickened
till he died,
Will sit again, and stand again, will run again and leap,
And of their death feel no more pain than we do when
we sleep.

PETER:    Will you stop your silly joking. We've been to a funeral.

SHEPERD:    To joke at death is shocking.

CUDDY:                    But it's true, God bless you all!
A man just came from Bethlehem, knocking at every
house,
And woke up all Jerusalem, the chickens and the cows.
They say in her conceiving that his mother stayed intact.

CHLOE:    That's not for my believing.

CUDDY:                     But, sweet lady, it's a fact.
Her husband, Joseph, swears it, and most surely he should
know.

PETER:    He has the horn and wears it, but he doesn't have to blow.

SHEPHERD:    Peter, catch him by the forelock so that I may feel his
pulse.
This is dementia precox.

73

CUDDY:                                        If you do, I'll crack your skulls.
          I will not take your medicine, I will not take your dose,
          And here's a kick upon the shin, a bang upon your nose.

[Exit CUDDY, *running, and enter* ROLAND *with the graveclothes still around him*]

SHEPHERD: God help us all, what is this now!

PETER:                                            Orestes, up again!

SHEPHERD: If I escape I make this vow, to leave off drink and women.

                                        [ROLAND *to the front*]

ROLAND:   I dreamed I died and rose through chilly space,
          And suddenly I felt the marrow lost
          Of pity, toleration, interest.
          The stony sun would never shed a tear,
          The moon like a mad girl went screaming by,
          I saw my funeral far, far below,
          And you as animals of a gray kind.
          The wolves would run a long way with your bones.

          Then, as the worms began their butchery,
          And as I hovered on a burning brink,
          I fell and trailed
          These linens down a comfortable sky,
          And was contained in hands, attended by
          An angel in a starry ambulance.
          My wool washed white,
          Straightway upon eternity I rushed.

          Then, then it was I heard the mourners cry
          The Sacrificial Lamb. This was not I,
          But someone else, it seemed. And soon I knew,
          For travelers arrived, a company,
          And one called Jesus, with bliss flickering
          From deep wounds that he wore. I heard them sing,
          And I too sang in tones of purest joy,
          For it was He, my master, bright Apollo,
          Though changed miraculously, gentler now.
          He turned toward me, and the singing stopped . . .

          I cannot quite remember what He said,
          But something that pertained to animals,

74

That he on whom the splendid vision falls
Will live again. The wool pulled from my eyes,
This death, I knew, was only a disguise,
And when my heart had almost burst for joy,
As from a dream woke smiling, still with tears.
So I returned from death, but cannot remember
The rest of the journey.

[*Enter* THE FURIES]

1ST FURY: Woe, woe, woe,
We have been betrayed,
Our kingdom is laid low
Even among the dead.
The law is not above
Nor is the law below.
I tear my garments so,
Put ashes on my head.

2ND FURY: Woe, woe, woe,
We have been betrayed,
But yet, before we go,
Tremble and be afraid.
These newer laws of love
Will shatter at a blow
The order that's above,
The order that's below.

3RD FURY: Woe, woe, woe,
We have been betrayed,
But centuries will show
The right of what we did.
The turning wheel will move
This Jesus out also,
And the event will prove
That truth is always so.

## SCENE FIVE

[PETER, ROLAND, CHLOE, CUDDY.]

PETER: I wish I could persuade you still to stay.

ROLAND: We'll meet again, dear Peter, some fine day.
But now that star will lead me to the child,
And I must seek him out. Be reconciled.

I've come a long way, there's a long way to go
Over the mountains, in the cold snow.

PETER: Wait till tomorrow. Surely Christ will keep.
He wouldn't grudge an animal his sleep.
Wait till the summer, when the sun has flecked
The olives. There's no hurry to a sect.
You've come a long way, there's a long way to go
Over the mountains, in the cold snow.

CHLOE: Yes, wait till summer, when the greening vines
Dance down the gentle valley in their lines,
When the glad shepherd pipes upon the hay
And the ewes bleat, and the young lambkins play.
You may change your mind. Wait till you know.
Think of the mountains and the cold snow.

PETER: See how the night, a smoky column, turns
In the cold wind, and the hard frost burns
The silent hills . . .

ROLAND:                               No more, for I must do
One certain thing. Good friends, goodbye to you.
My mind is made up, and now I must go
Over the mountains, in the cold snow.

But, in my turn, may I invite you all . . .

PETER: No thank you, Roland, my poor lambs would bawl,
And I don't trust this child of whom you speak,
The way is roundabout, the prospect bleak,
This may be just a fashion, more or less.
I do not think that I will go, I guess.
I am afraid he may turn out a snob
Who never has a wife or holds a job.
No, I'll be total in each enterprise,
And after, make my vices meet my eyes.

[*Enter* CUDDY, *running*]

CUDDY: I have given up my business and left my family,
For where the star has risen is the place where I would
    be.
I will cross the Jordan river in a carillon of bells,
Though it's cold I will not shiver, He will take away my
    spells.

76

He will take your sins away at once, so be no more
    perplexed,
He's the pause between what happens and the thing that
    happens next.

ROLAND:     Now let the bottoms of the precipices
Reëcho these immortal promises,
And let the mountains tell through all their ranges
That death itself is changed, that all things changes.
And now we are off, there's a long way to go
Over the mountains, in the cold snow.

                                            [*Exeunt* ROLAND *and* CUDDY.]


CHLOE:      Goodbye, dear Roland, and good luck to you.
PETER:      This is good news of death, if it is true.

## THE END

PETER's emblem: *Absit invidia.*
ROLAND's emblem: *Non omnis moriar.*

# A Dream of Governors
## 1959

# The Green Shepherd

Here sit a shepherd and a shepherdess,
He playing on his melancholy flute;
The sea wind ruffles up her simple dress
And shows the delicacy of her foot.

And there you see Constantinople's wall
With arrows and Greek fire, molten lead;
Down from a turret seven virgins fall,
Hands folded, each one praying on her head.

The shepherd yawns and puts his flute away.
It's time, she murmurs, we were going back.
He offers certain reasons she should stay—
But neither sees the dragon on their track.

A dragon like a car in a garage
Is in the wood, his long tail sticking out.
Here rides St. George, swinging his sword and targe,
And sticks the grinning dragon in the snout.

Puffing a smoke ring, like the cigarette
Over Times Square, Sir Dragon snorts his last.
St. George takes off his armor in a sweat.
The Middle Ages have been safely passed.

What is the sail that crosses the still bay,
Unnoticed by the shepherds? It could be
A caravel that's sailing to Cathay,
Westward from Palos on the unknown sea.

But the green shepherd travels in her eye
And whispers nothings in his lady's ear,
And sings a little song, that roses die,
*Carpe Diem*, which she seems pleased to hear.

The vessel they ignored still sails away
So bravely on the water, Westward Ho!
And murdering, in a religious way,
Brings Jesus to the Gulf of Mexico.

Now Portugal is fading, and the state
Of Castile rising purple on Peru;

Now England, now America grows great—
With which these lovers have nothing to do.

What do they care if time, uncompassed, drift
To China, and the crew is a baboon?
But let him whisper always, and her lift
The oceans in her eyelids to the moon.

The dragon rises crackling in the air,
And who is god but Dagon? Wings careen,
Rejoicing, on the Russian hemisphere.
Meanwhile, the shepherd dotes upon her skin.

Old Aristotle, having seen this pass,
From where he studied in the giant's cave,
Went in and shut his book and locked the brass
And lay down with a shudder in his grave.

The groaning pole had gone more than a mile;
These shepherds did not feel it where they loved,
For time was sympathetic all the while
And on the magic mountain nothing moved.

# I Dreamed that in a City Dark as Paris

I dreamed that in a city dark as Paris
I stood alone in a deserted square.
The night was trembling with a violet
Expectancy. At the far edge it moved
And rumbled; on that flickering horizon
The guns were pumping color in the sky.

There was the Front. But I was lonely here,
Left behind, abandoned by the army.
The empty city and the empty square
Was my inhabitation, my unrest.
The helmet with its vestige of a crest,
The rifle in my hands, long out of date,
The belt I wore, the trailing overcoat
And hobnail boots, were those of a *poilu*.
I was the man, as awkward as a bear.

Over the rooftops where cathedrals loomed
In speaking majesty, two aeroplanes
Forlorn as birds, appeared. Then growing large,
The German *Taube* and the *Nieuport Scout*,
They chased each other tumbling through the sky,
Till one streamed down on fire to the earth.

These wars have been so great, they are forgotten
Like the Egyptian dynasts. My confrere
In whose thick boots I stood, were you amazed
To wander through my brain four decades later
As I have wandered in a dream through yours?

The violence of waking life disrupts
The order of our death. Strange dreams occur,
For dreams are licensed as they never were.

# A Dream of Governors

*The deepest dream is of mad governors.*
MARK VAN DOREN

The Knight from the world's end
Cut off the dragon's head.
The monster's only friend,
The Witch, insulting, fled.
The Knight was crowned, and took
His Lady. Good and gay,
They lived in a picture book
Forever and a day.

Or else: When he had sat
So long, the King was old
And ludicrous and fat.
At feasts when poets told
How he had shed the blood
Of dragons long ago
He thought, Have I done good
To hear that I did so?

The chorus in a play
Declaimed: "The soul does well
Keeping the middle way."
He thought, That city fell;
Man's life is founded on
Folly at the extreme;
When all is said and done
The City is a dream.

At night the King alone
Went to the dragon's cave.
In moonlight on a stone
The Witch sat by the grave.
He grasped her by the hand
And said, "Grant what I ask.
Bring evil on the land
That I may have a task!"

The Queen has heard his tread;
She shuts the picture book.
The King stands by the bed.
In silence as they look
Into each other's eyes
They see a buried thing
That creeps, begins to rise,
And spreads the dragon's wing.

# Orpheus in the Underworld

Night, dark night, night of my distress—
The moon is glittering with all the tears
Of the long silence and unhappiness
Of those who loved in vain for many years.

And so it glittered on the sleeping town
When Orpheus alone and sadly went
To death, to fetch Eurydice, and down
The fearful road pursued his dark descent.

Here were the walls, the gates where death had set
His warnings—in a city carved in stone
The citizens were busy; farmers whet
Their scythes in meadows never to be mown.

The kings and judges sat in their high places.
Then, at the sound of a loud trumpet blown,
They crowded, with pale terror on their faces,
From Death ascending to his dreadful throne.

Orpheus entered. As the eery light
Dwindled, he grasped his lute, and stumbling bent
His footsteps through the thick, enshrouding night.
Then suddenly, the lute by accident

Was struck—the sound exploded like a star
And shone and faded, and the Echoes woke
And danced, and ran before him. Down the far
Corridors it seemed the silence spoke.

He touched the strings again, began to play
In the same order. Fearfully he went
Toward the Echoes, and they still gave way.
And so he followed his own instrument.

At last to the deep hall of death he came.
And there the King sat, motionless and dread.
The night coiled from his nostrils like a flame;
The eyes lacked luster in the massive head.

And by his icy feet, pale in her shroud,
The beautiful Eurydice was laid.

Orpheus knelt beside her, and he bowed
His head, and touched the lute again, and played.

Night, dark night, night of my distress—
Once by the Mediterranean in May
I heard a nightingale, and the sadness of roses
In the murmuring wind, but this was sadder than they.

Night, dark night, night of my distress—
I too have waked her, seen the heavy shawl
Of night slip from her shoulders, and the darkness
Fly from her open eyes. And through the hall,

Through cities and the country of the dead
With the one I loved, hand in hand, have gone.
The dog of death was quiet as we fled,
And so we passed, as shadows over stone.

Under the hills in their enormous silence
And by the sea where it is always still,
I felt her hand in mine, the fearful sense
Of mortal love. And so we fled, until

I turned toward her. With a cry she vanished.
Goodbye, pale shadow of my happiness!
I to the light have been forever banished
That is the night, the night of my distress.

Then Orpheus pursued his lonely way
Upward into the world, and a strange glory
Shone from his face. The trees, when he would play,
Were moved, and roses wept to hear his story.

It's Orpheus in the wind. His music grieves
The moon. He tells the water of his loss.
And all the birds are silent, and the leaves
Of summer in that music sigh and toss.

# The Flight to Cytherea

There are designs in curtains that can kill,
Insidious intentions in a chair;
In conversation, silence, sitting still,
The demon of decorum and despair.

Once, when I felt like that, I used to go
Abroad. I've made my marches drunk on night,
Hands in my pockets, pipe sparks flying so,
A liner to the tropics of the light.

Night is the people's theater, sad and droll.
There are the lovers, leaning on each other;
The businessmen, out for a little stroll
With their success; the bum who calls you brother.

And then, I've flown. I've risen like a sail,
A plane—the roads beneath shone bright and bare—
A black umbrella cracking in the gale
Over an ocean blank as a nightmare.

And came to Paris. I'm not talking of
Your chestnut blossoms, but the soldier's town,
The Butte, the calvados, odors of love,
Where for a little while I settled down.

In Africa I was. Beneath my wings
The lions roared. I floated on tobacco;
I made the eyeballs of the savage kings
Roll up. I spent a fortune at Monaco.

Then off again, to heights where the air fails,
The Alps are only shadows to the West,
That patch is India, the den of whales
A puddle—ecstasies on Everest!

And glided out beyond the atmosphere
Toward the moon. It trembled like a bell.
"Step right up, gentlemen!" Then sudden fear
Opened. I felt the precipice. I fell.

Down down like an umbrella I unfurled
My bones. I must have fallen for a week;

Then slowly and more slowly as the world
Unwrinkled, valley, plain, and mountain peak.

And fell into the country of your eyes,
Since when I have lived comfortably here;
My thoughts are only clouds in summer skies,
And everything is perfect, calm and clear.

# To the Western World

A siren sang, and Europe turned away
From the high castle and the shepherd's crook.
Three caravels went sailing to Cathay
On the strange ocean, and the captains shook
Their banners out across the Mexique Bay.

And in our early days we did the same.
Remembering our fathers in their wreck
We crossed the sea from Palos where they came
And saw, enormous to the little deck,
A shore in silence waiting for a name.

The treasures of Cathay were never found.
In this America, this wilderness
Where the axe echoes with a lonely sound,
The generations labor to possess
And grave by grave we civilize the ground.

# Hot Night on Water Street

A hot midsummer night on Water Street—
The boys in jeans were combing their blond hair,
Watching the girls go by on tired feet;
And an old woman with a witch's stare
Cried "Praise the Lord!" She vanished on a bus
With hissing air brakes, like an incubus.

Three hardware stores, a barbershop, a bar,
A movie playing Westerns—where I went
To see a dream of horses called *The Star*. . . .
Some day, when this uncertain continent
Is marble, and men ask what was the good
We lived by, dust may whisper "Hollywood."

Then back along the river bank on foot
By moonlight. . . . On the West Virginia side
An owlish train began to huff and hoot;
It seemed to know of something that had died.
I didn't linger—sometimes when I travel
I think I'm being followed by the Devil.

At the newsstand in the lobby, a cigar
Was talkative: "Since I've been in this town
I've seen one likely woman, and a car
As she was crossing Main Street, knocked her down."
I was a stranger here myself, I said,
And bought the *New York Times*, and went to bed.

# The Boarder

The time is after dinner. Cigarettes
      Glow on the lawn;
Glasses begin to tinkle; TV sets
      Have been turned on.

The moon is brimming like a glass of beer
      Above the town,
And love keeps her appointments—"Harry's here!"
      "I'll be right down."

But the pale stranger in the furnished room
      Lies on his back
Looking at paper roses, how they bloom,
      And ceilings crack.

# Orpheus in America

Here are your meadows, Love, as wide as heaven,
Green spirits, leaves
And winds, your ministers!

Item: a ship, that on the outer shoals
Lies broken. Item: thirty-seven souls,
Or rather, thirty-seven kinds of fever.
Item: three Indians, chained leg to leg.
Item: my lute.

This is the New England—rocks and brush
Where none may live but only tigers, parrots,
And mute imagining—
America, a desert with a name.

America begins antiquity.
Confronted with pure space, my Arcady
Has turned to stone.
Rome becomes Rome; Greece, Greece; the cottages
Collapse in ruin.

It darkens like a lapse of memory.
Here are no palaces, but lifted stone,
The pyramids of Egypt, steles
Of Ur. Columns that death has set
At the entrance to his kingdom.


## II

This gazing freedom is the basilisk.
O for a mirror!
The melancholy of the possible
Unmeasures me.

Let music then begin. And let the air
Be passing sweet,
Music that scarcely wakes
The serpent in her trance
And leads the lion out into the dance.

93

And let the trees be moved,
And may the forest dance.

Then shall intelligence and grace
Join hands and sing: Goodbye to Arcady!
Another world is here, a greener Thrace!
Here are your meadows, Love, as wide as heaven,
Green spirits, leaves
And winds, your ministers,
In this America, this other, happy place.

# An American in the Thieves' Market

In Italy the dead have all the passion.
They still reverberate among the broken
Columns and stones. And in comparison
    The living seem
Content, in the light-garlanded piazza,
To stare at beauty, strolling with no aim
Between the silly fountains and the dim
    Forgetful stream.

If I were an Italian, I'd pinch
Life on the thigh—*"Buon giorno!"*—with a smile.
This is my business day: the offered bribe,
    Which I decline,
Then pocket—putting something in the glove
Of the police. At noon, enough of this.
And my old age is gazing, with my mistress,
    Cigars and wine.

But I am American, and bargain
In the Thieves' Market, where the junk of culture
Lies in the dust—clay shards, perhaps Etruscan,
    And wedding rings . . .
My father's ghost is ticking in a watch,
My mother's, weeping in the antique bed,
And, in a pile of swords, my cousins shed
    The tears of things.

# Music in Venice

Dismiss the instruments that for your pleasure
Have played allegro all through Italy.
Pay the musicians. Even let the poet
        Have part his pay.
For here is Venice—floating, and suspended
From purple clouds. Dismiss the music school!
Here anyone at all can play the fool
        In his own way.

Then thread the labyrinth of narrow streets,
Bridges, canals, windows of lace and glass,
High lattices that spill the scent of almonds.
        The Minotaur
That lurks in this maze is kind. An Aschenbach
Round every corner is pursuing Eros.
"Love!" cry the naked offspring of the heroes
        On the wet stone floor.

It's night in the Piazza. Lighted space
Burns like your brandy. Violins and brass
Play waltzes, fox-trots. On a cloud, St. Mark's
        Winged lion perches;
High palaces go sailing to the moon,
Which, as advertised, is perfectly clear.
The lovers rise, moon-struck, and whisper their
        *Arrivedercis.*

A prince of Venice, tangled in the eyes
Of a young courtesan, once staged a masque:
"The Banishment of Love." A boy like Eros
        Was rowed in chains,
Weeping, down the canal. The merchant's Venice
Splintered the Turk and swept him from her shores.
But Eros came, Eros with many oars,
        And Eros reigns.

Venice, the city built on speculation,
Still stands on it. Love sails from India
And Sweden—every hanging cloud pours out
        A treasure chest.

It's love on the Rialto, news of love,
That gives Antonio his golden life,
Even to Envy, sharpening a knife,
    His interest.

# Côte d'Azur

Christian says, "You know, it's Paradise,"
Mending his net.
"The English," he says, "for example . . .
They come and lie in the sun until they are
As red as that roof.
And then it's finished. They never recover."

The howling native children,
Roland, Giorgio, Josette, plunge in the sea,
Scramble on a raft, inspect
The official from Lyons with his glass rod
And nylon gear.
    "I know," Roland informs him,
"Where you could have bought all that much cheaper.
That's not much of a rod."
      "And you,"
Replies the head of the bureau
To his tormentor, "What kind of a rod
Do *you* have?"
    Roland shrugs.
"Me?" he says. "I don't have all that money."

And here comes an excursion *en famille*.
First, they erect a yellow canvas tent
Which swallows them. Then mama-pig comes out
On her white trotters; whining daughter-pig;
Boy-pig and Baby. Look, the blossoming
Of beach-umbrellas, uncollapsing of chairs!
And last emerges the head of the family,
His face encased in glass, his feet
Froglike in flippers.
Out of his head a kind of man-from-Mars
Tube curls; his right hand grasps a trident
For finding the sea urchin. *Me voici!*

Here and there on the beach the solitary
Brood in the sun—Dutchman and Swede;
An actress in dark glasses
Reading a book; heroes and heroines

Of melodramas that are to be played:
The shot in the hotel; the speech
From a platform; the performance
Of Bach that brings the audience to their feet
Roaring in Dusseldorf.

Humankind, says the poet, cannot bear
Too much reality.
                  Nor pleasure.
And nothing is more melancholy
Than to watch people enjoying themselves
As much as they can.
                  The trick is to be busy
Mending your net, like Christian,
Or active as the father is out there
With all his tackle.

                  Look! he's caught
An octopus.

                  The children come running,
And even the Swede
Stands up to look; the actress
Smiles; and the official from Lyons
Forgets himself in the general excitement.

# The Runner

*This is the story of a soldier of the 101st Airborne Division of the Army of the United States.*

*The Runner is fiction; the episodes and characters are imaginary. But the fiction is based on the following history.*

*On September 17, 1944, parachute and glider infantry of the First British Airborne Division, the American 82nd and 101st Airborne Divisions, and a Polish brigade, descended in eastern Holland, at Eindhoven, Grave, Nijmegen, and Arnhem. Their object was to make a bridgehead across the Lower Rhine at Arnhem. The British Second Army would join them and advance from Arnhem into the plains of northern Germany.*

*At Arnhem the British airborne troops were attacked by enemy units in overwhelming strength, and forced back across the river. The more fortunate Americans defended a corridor from Eindhoven to Nijmegen. The fighting, bitter at first, settled into a stalemate, and, with the coming of the rainy season, petered out entirely.*

*In mid-November the 82nd and 101st were drawn back to Rheims, to re-equip and get the drizzle out of their bones.*

*On December 17, they were alerted for combat. A German attack was developing in Belgium. The divisions were hurried by truck into the Ardennes, and on the night of December 19, the 101st were digging in around Bastogne.*

*This poem is for Donald Hall who encouraged me to write it.*


## I

"And the condemned man ate a hearty meal,"
The runner said. He took his mess kit over
To the garbage can. He scraped his mess kit out,
Then dipped it in the can of soapy water,
And swished it in the can of clean, hot water,
And came back to his place.

           The company
Was spread along one edge of the airfield,
Finishing lunch. Those with the appetite
Were going through the chow line once again.
They looked all pockets, pockets and baggy pants.
They held their mess kits out to the sweating cooks,

Who filled them up; then bore their precious load
Apart.

      The runner felt in his breast pocket
For cigarettes. He lit one and inhaled.
Leaning back on his pack, his feet sprawled out,
He stared at the ranks of gliders and towplanes
And said, "I wonder if . . ."

              "Agh!" said a voice,
"Why don't you dry up, Dodd!"

                 He looked around
And met the eyes of Kass, the radioman,
Glaring beneath the rim of his steel helmet.

"What?" said the runner.

          "Who needs your remarks?
First, the condemned men eat a hearty meal,
And then you wonder . . ."

          "When we're coming back."

"What's it to you?"

        The runner didn't answer.
Sometimes it seemed that anything he said
Rubbed someone the wrong way. He'd only meant
He hoped the outfit would come back to England.
He liked the village where they had been quartered,
And London, where he'd gone on two-day passes.
He liked the pubs, the mugs of mild-and-bitter,
And country lanes. Some day, when they came back,
He'd go off on his own. Rent a bicycle.
He'd see some of the country by himself.
And if he got to London . . .

          With a roar
An engine started. Other engines followed.
A gale from the propellers swept around him.

"Fall in!" said the First Sergeant.

           Dodd got up
And hoisted on his pack.

       "Get a move on!"

That's how it was: you always had to wait,
And then you had to hurry. He closed his belt,
And slung his rifle over his right shoulder.
The section formed.

              "Where's Wheeler?" said the sergeant.
And here came Wheeler at a run. "You, Wheeler . . ."
The sergeant followed him with imprecations
As Wheeler ducked in place at Dodd's right hand.
Out of the side of his mouth: "Look what I got,"
Said Wheeler, and he showed in his clenched fist
A bundle of the new invasion money.
"Over in F Company," he whispered.
"The dice was really hot."

              "Ten-*hut!* For-*ard*
*Arch!*" said the sergeant, and they started off
Across the concrete runway. It seemed long.
Dodd's mouth was dry; his legs were weak. At last
They came up to the glider, their box kite—
High wings and rudder, little wheels that hardly
Lifted it off the ground—a canvas coffin.
Ungainly as a duck, it wouldn't fly
Unless it had to.

              Through the open door
Under the wing, they climbed up one by one,
Toppling with their burdens. Found their seats.
And sat in two rows, looking at each other.
Dodd fastened his safety belt and clasped his gun
Between his knees. The Captain entered last.
They waited. The glider trembled in the blast
Of wind from the towplane. The pilots entered,
Leaping up lightly, and made their way forward
To the controls.

              The runner could see nothing
Beyond the glider's high, transparent nose;
But now, he thought, the towplane would be turning
Into the wind. Two men would run the cable
Back from the plane and hook it to the glider.
Then, with a louder blast of the propellers,
The plane would start to roll.

                    The glider jerked
Forward, and rolled, creaking, and gathered speed.
The bumping stopped, and with a sudden lightness
They were airborne. Constricted where he sat,
Dodd prayed to nothing in particular:
Let the rope hold; no current whirl us down
Smashing on concrete.

                    They were well away.
He stared at the slender pilots in their pinks
And sporty caps and glasses; at their hands
On the half-wheel. His life was in those hands.
He thought of shell bursts, the green canvas torn,
Men writhing in their belts, the pilots' hands
Fallen from the controls, a sickening drop.
And then he thought of fields with pointed stakes
That would shear through the sides. Of plunging out
Into machine-gun fire.


          II

                    "We're almost there,"
The next man said.

                    The pilots were peering down.
One nodded, and the other raised his hand
And grasped the lever that released the cable,
And pulled it down.

                    The glider soared, then fell
Slanting away. The wing rose up again.
They glided down on silence and the wind.

The fields were rushing at them, tilted steep.
Dodd braced himself. The glider leveled, lightly
Bumped on the ground, and rolled to a dead stop.

The door was open. They were climbing through.
And now were standing in an open field
Flat as a pancake. Gliders strewed the scene.
Others were skimming down; and still the sky
Was filled with gliders.

From their lifted bows
The gliders were disgorging jeeps and cannon.
Riflemen formed their files and marched away.
Dodd's section took its place in the company.
The Captain raised his arm; he swept it down,
And they were marching.

On the bright horizon
A windmill stood. The land was crossed with dykes.
It looked like a Dutch painting. To their left
A wood began. They marched in that direction.

The day was hot, and Dodd began to sweat.
Then to his ears came the familiar sound
Of guns, the battle-roll, continuous.
Then all his other days were like a dream.
This was reality: the heat, the load
Strapping his shoulder, and the sound of guns.

The war, after Normandy, had seemed remote.
He had been there; his courage had been proved
To his own satisfaction. He had listened
To talk about the fighting, and he'd talked
And lost the sense of truth. He had forgotten
The smell of apples and the fear of death.
Now he remembered. And it seemed unjust
That he should be required to survive
Again. The sound increased. The battleground
Looked ominous. Visions of a huge mistake
Struck at his heart.

### III

The company was entering the woods.

"Dodd," said the sergeant, "take this message up
To Lieutenant Farr."

He stepped out of the file
And hastened to the front. The lead platoon
Was walking slowly, with the scouts ahead.
He gave the message.

"Right," said the lieutenant.
The runner started back. As he went by

Faces stared into his inquiringly.
He seemed possessed of an important secret.

Shots went off behind him. He crouched and swung
Out of the path, and lay in the scrub, face down.
The firing stopped. A voice was calling "Medic!"

Fisher, a sergeant of the third platoon,
Came up the path, bent low. He shook Dodd's shoulder:
"Who's doing all the shooting?"

                              "*I* don't know,"
Dodd said. The sergeant, with a grim expression,
Stared at him, and went on.

                         The runner waited.
Why didn't they get it over with!

                         "Move out!"

He got to his feet. The path filled up with men.
He made his way back, past the sweating faces
Now streaked with dust. He fell in with his section,
Turned round, and traveled up the path again
He'd just traversed.

                    The files ahead were parting.
The men looked down, as into a precipice.
There was a body lying in the way.
It was Santelli, of the first platoon.
Dodd had just seen him going out in front;
He walked like a dancer, with a short, neat step,
Rifle held crosswise.

                    He lay huddled up
On his left side; his helmet had rolled off;
His head was seeping blood out in the dirt.

The files ahead were lagging; then they hurried.
"Keep your intervals!" the Captain shouted.
They hated him together.

                        At the break
They sprawled out of the path, in the underbrush.
Santelli's death had made them strangely silent.
Their helmets bowed their heads down on their chests.

Under the distant thudding of the guns,
The weight of all their burdens and the sky,
They couldn't speak, or stir themselves, or lift
A cigarette.

       Dodd thought about Santelli.
One of the afternoons it seemed forever
All they would do was practice for the war
With marches, tactics, and map exercises,
He lay beneath the wall of an English garden,
Sucking a stalk of grass, and watched the clouds,
And far above the clouds, a fleet of bombers
Trailing long plumes of white across the blue.
Close by, Santelli sat, paring his nails
With a pocketknife

       "Hey, runner-boy," he said
In the familiar and sneering tone
That Dodd despised. "What're we doin, hey?
You've been to college, right?" His little eyes
Were sharp with mockery—a little man
Of pocketknives and combs. "You ought to know.
What's it all about?"


       IV

A plane flew glittering out of the sun—
A *Thunderbolt*. It swooped and disappeared
Behind a screen of trees. Then a staccato
Sound began. Machine guns. The plane rose
And flew away. They watched it till it vanished.

"On your feet," the sergeant said.

       "My aching back!"
Someone said; but the gripe lacked conviction.
They stood and crumbled out their cigarettes,
And rolled the paper into little balls,
As though they'd like to keep the battlefield
Clean as a barracks.

       As Dodd marched, the weight
Sawed at his shoulders: pack and ammunition,

Gas mask and trench tool, bayonet, grenades.
He plodded with clenched jaws, his eyes cast down
On the dusty path, the heels moving ahead.
He stayed, it seemed, in a fixed position;
It was the scene that moved.

                              The path reeled in
Another corpse. It came to him boot-first:
A German soldier on his back, spread-eagle,
A big, fresh-blooded, blond, jack-booted man
In dusty gray. Stepping around the fingers,
Around the bucket helmet, Dodd stared down.
A fly lit on the teeth. He looked away
And to the front, where other attitudes
Of death were waiting. He assumed them all,
One by one, in his imagination,
In order to prevent them.

                              Small-arms fire
Was crackling through the wood. Platoons spread out
In arrow-shaped formations.

                    "Dig in!"

                              He dug.
The shovel sank in sand; he hacked at roots.
Overhead, shells were whispering, and smoke
Came drifting back.

                    Two planes went whistling over.
*Typhoons*. They darted searching on the front.
They dived, and from their wings plunged rockets down
In smoking streaks. The ground shook with concussions.

"We're moving out!"

                    Dodd climbed out of the hole
That he had dug. The company moved in silence
Through the burning wood.


                    V

Beyond the wood there stretched an open road.
They filed out on it. In a field of hay

A plane perched on its nose, a *Messerschmidt*,
The black cross glaring.

                      Houses stood here and there.
In front of one, a mattress had been laid,
And on the mattress, a German officer.
He was puffed up with air like a balloon,
Belly and limbs swelling as if to split
His uniform. The grass was stuck with feathers.

Night was falling; the light had left the fields.
The road approached a village. At the entrance
A German half-track had been blown apart,
Its mustard-yellow metal torn and scorched;
Out of it spilled the crew, burned black as rubber.
The street, as they passed through, was strewn with dead,
A presentation of boot soles and teeth,
Letters, cigars, the contents of their lives.

The cannonading was more loud, and flashes
Lit the darkening sky. A company
Of paratroopers passed them, coming back
With somber faces.

## VI

Night. And the fields were still. The cannonade
Was flickering and grumbling through the sky.
Red flashes lined the clouds. No breath of wind
Was moving. In the holes that they had dug
The tired troops were sleeping on their arms.

"Dodd, get up!"

                He struggled out of his bag.

The First Sergeant leaned over: "Take this message
Back to Battalion."

              Dodd took the paper,
His helmet and his M–1, and set off,
Still half asleep.

              Darkness without a moon
Surrounded him. He made his lonely way

Over a road that skirted trees and dykes.
The guns were rumbling; shells went fluttering over;
Machine-gun tracers sparkled distantly.
A flare popped in the sky and glimmered down;
He waited in the shadow of a tree
Till it went out. And took the road again.

A deepening of black, a looming wall,
Was Battalion C. P. The guard called out:
"Halt! Who's there?"

               The runner spoke the password:
"Kansas!" and was admitted by the guard
Into the courtyard. There he gave his message
To a tech-sergeant; sat down on a bench,
And waited, looking at the pulsing sky.

"Runner!"

       He answered.

            "Take this message back."

That was his job. Now all I need, he thought,
Is one of those Philip Morris uniforms
The bellboys wear.

           The road was long and dark.
And it was weird to be alone in Holland
At midnight on this road. As he went on
He felt he had no weight. The landscape seemed
To have more things to think of than his journey.
These errands gave him little satisfaction.
Some men might think he led the life of Riley,
Safe and warm and dry, around Headquarters.
A man could be a runner all his life
And never be shot at. That's what they thought.
But how about the shelling? He'd been shelled
As much as anyone. And back in France,
At Carentan, he had been shot at—plenty!
It wasn't his fault he never had a chance
To fire back. Now, right here on this road,
He might be killed by accident. But still,
That wouldn't be the same as being brave.

He had no chance to be thought so, no part
In the society of riflemen.
So, as he went, he reasoned with himself.


VII

Next day the company went up on line
Near Veghel. They were digging round a church,
In the cemetery, and were just knee-deep
When hell broke loose.

                    The screaming and flat crack
Of eighty-eights.

              Airbursts.

                    The metal slashed
The trees and ricocheted. Bit in the ground.

The runner on his belly lay contracting
Under the edge of metal. From a tree
A yard away, leaves flew.

                    A voice cried "Medic!"

His belly and his buttocks clenched each time
A shell came in. And they kept coming in.
He felt a sting between his shoulder blades.
I'm wounded! he thought, with a rush of joy.

"Dodd!" someone called.

                    He went on hands and knees
Toward the voice.

                    "Over here," it urged him.

It was his sergeant, with a dozen cases
Of mortar shells.

                    "Take them up to the mortars,"
The sergeant said. "They're out of ammunition."

He took two cases, one beneath each arm,
And ran off, dodging among the trees and graves.
He found the mortars and came running back
To get another load. The crack and hum

Of the artillery was all around him.
He felt the sting of the place where he'd been hit.
He knew that he was brave.

On the last trip,
Kneeling above a mortar, as he lowered
The cases gently, one of the mortar crew
Said, "You're a good man, Dodd."

That night he lay
Smiling, without a care, beneath the sky.
He had done all that could be expected.


## VIII

October, and the sky was turning gray.
The battle line had settled. Every night
The bombers flew, going to Germany
At a great height. And back the other way
The V–1's came. The soldiers in their holes
Heard them droning and saw the rhythmic flames
Carrying woe to Antwerp and to England.

They dozed or watched. Then it began to rain,
And always rained. It seemed they were never dry.
Winter was in the air. Paths turned to mud.
By day and night the shells came shrieking in;
They got so they could tell a dying fall
And pay the rest no mind. They lived with mud.
They cooked and ate their rations in the can,
And tried to dry their socks between two rains.
Cold and sullen, under a raincoat roof,
They shivered in their holes.

One moonlit night
Dodd was returning on his way alone.
There was a wind; the haunted shadows stirred,
And rainpools glimmered in the moonlit fields.

There was a field the runner loathed to cross.
A place of horrors. Here, on the first day,
There'd been fierce charges, combats at close range,
And the dead were mixed as they had fallen.

Here crouched the German soldier with his *schmeisser*
Close to the parachutist in his rage—
Putrid things, never to be forgotten.
The field was swelling, shining with an aura
Of pale corruption.

        To avoid it, Dodd
Went by another path he did not know,
Leading, it seemed, back to the company.
But in a while a fearful premonition
Stopped him. In a shadow, cold with dread,
He stood listening. The branches stirred,
And all at once there was a clash of arms,
The sounds of footsteps. Stealthily he turned
To slip away.

        *"Wer geht da?"*

        He ran.
He plunged into the darkness, blind with panic.
A storm of shots erupted at his back.
Brambles tore at his legs. He climbed a bank,
Clawing, and stumbled down the other side.
Then, as he ran, he shouted out the password:
"Ohio!" like a dog drenched with hot water.
His rifle fell. He left it where it was.
"Ohio!" He collided with a branch
And staggered. At his back the storm increased.
Red tracers streaked the air. Across a ditch
He leaped. And ran across the road beyond.
A hole was in his way; he cleared it with
A stride, and the dark figure starting up
Out of the hole. He kept on running, shouting
"Ohio!" A shape standing in the path
Snatched at him; he swerved out of its grasp.
There was a maze of holes. He stumbled, reeled,
And fell. His helmet flew off with a clang.

Feet were approaching. He lay still as death.
"It's Dodd," said a voice.

        At last, he looked up
Into the faces of the third platoon.
Fisher. Others. They looked down in wonder.

# IX

The regiment was bivouacked near Rheims
In tents on the bare plain. Wind-driven clouds
Streamed over, and the land in chilly streaks
Heaved like a sea. The wind hummed on the ropes
And whipped the tent flaps.

                Dodd, stretched on his cot,
Could see and hear the third platoon at drill.
They turned to the flank and to the flank again;
They marched to the rear.

              "Count cadence . . . cadence count!"

"*Hup* . . . two . . . three . . . four!" they answered on the wind.
The sun flashed from the slanting rifle butts.

The corporal shouted: "When I say Ohio,
To the rear march, and double-time like hell!"
There was a burst of laughter, then: "Ohio!
Run!" the corporal said, "*Hup* . . . two . . . three . . . four!
Halt! Now we'll try that movement once again.
When I give the word Ohio, turn around
And double-time as if your name is Dodd.
Make it look good. All right now—forward *'arch!*
Ohio!"

        Dodd rolled over on his face.
He saw himself once more before the Captain:
"Screaming the password . . . throwing away your gun . . .
Keep out of my sight, Dodd. You make me sick."

And then, the jokes, from reveille to sleep:
"That is Ohio, one of the midwest boys."
Replacements would be sent to see Ohio
To draw their running shoes. "I'm from Cleveland,"
One of them told him. "What part are you from?"

He turned upon his back. Right overhead
His jacket hung, with regimental ribbons,
The bronze star, and his shameful purple heart.
He stared at it. If he could only sleep
The time between, until the sergeant came
To put him on another hard detail!

That was his punishment: to dig latrines,
Pick cigarette butts up, scrub greasy pots—
Or to do nothing for a live-long day
But think and try to read, in a cold tent.

When the men came in, they would ignore him—

"You going in to town?"

                    "You said it, man!"

Polishing up their paratrooper boots
Until the toes reflected a lit match;
Blousing the trousers in their boot tops; brushing
Their jackets; tucking ties between two buttons;
Cocking their caps—

          "Let's go!"

                    He fell asleep,
And dreamed that he was climbing. On the crest
A dummy stood, with stiff, ballooning arms
And painted face, in Prussian uniform.
He reached the arms and swung them. It went "B-r-r-r-m!"
Like a machine gun. "B-r-r-r-m!" the sound came out
The dummy's painted lips and barrel belly.
Then he was walking over a green field.
It was a country he had never seen,
With haystacks, a warm wind, and distant barns.
Shadows were walking with him, and a voice
Spoke with the measure of a travelogue:
"*Vingtième Division* . . . fifty per cent . . ."
Another voice inquired: "Casualties?"
"No," said the first voice, "all of them are dead."
And it continued: "*Douzième Infanterie* . . .
Fifty per cent . . ." As the first voice was speaking,
Over the field, as on a movie screen,
Hands were imposed; they held a scarlet cloth
And folded it. "René de Gaumartin,"
The voice continued, "Cardinal of France."
Again the hands were folding a red robe.
"Marcel Gaumartin, Cardinal of France."
And as the voice and the pale hands continued
Their meditative play, Dodd came upon

A girl in black. She had fair hair and skin,
Plain features, almost ugly, but her eyes
Were large, they shot out tender rays of light.
The voice said, "Mademoiselle de Maintenon."
In his dream, Dodd laughed. *De Maintenon!* She said,
In a voice remote with sadness, "Yes," and smiled,
"I try not to think of them too much."

                                He woke,
And his heart was light. It was a vision,
He thought. What does it mean? What eyes she had!
That field, with the wind blowing, and the clouds!
And yet, it was absurd. The words were nonsense.

He went out of his tent.

                      The third platoon
Were sitting down, taking a smoking break.
"Ohio!" someone shouted. "Where you running?"

He walked the other way, toward a rise
With trees, the only trees in all the plain,
Leaving the tents behind.

                        He climbed the slope
And sat beneath a tree. On the horizon
Rheims, with the cathedral, like a ship
Traveled the plain. Clouds were streaming over
The spire; their swift shadows ran like waves.
He lit a cigarette. Then, near at hand,
He saw the earth was trenched. A long depression,
No more than a foot deep, with rotten posts
And scraps of wire, wound across the slope.
He stood, and walked along it. The earth gave
Under his boots. He picked up a small scrap
Of wire, and it crumbled. He surmised
This was a trench dug in the first Great War.
Who knew? Perhaps an older war than that.
He faced the East, to Germany and Russia.
Shadows were standing with him. It was cold.
They watched, wrapped in old overcoats, forgotten.
They stamped their feet. The whole world was deserted
Except for them; there was nobody left.

On the imagined parapet, a cross
Howled in the wind; and there were photographs
Of girls and children; bunches of cut flowers.
Then, on the pitted, gaunt escarp, the night,
The melancholy night, swept with grandeur.
Far in the dark, star shells were blossoming.
They stamped their feet. It was too cold. Too much
To expect of them. Their boots sank in the mud.
Their veins seemed ice; their jaws creaked with the cold.
They spoke; their words were carried on the wind,
Mingled, and lost.

               But now, an actual sound
Arrived distinctly. When he turned to look,
The camp was stirring; men ran to and fro.
He saw the third platoon halt in their drill,
Fall out, and run toward their tents. He moved;
He ground his cigarette out underfoot,
And hastened down the slope.

                    "Where have you been?"
Said the First Sergeant.

                  "I've been for a walk.
What's going on?"

                  "Full field. Ready to move
In half an hour."

                Dodd's tent was in confusion.
The men were cramming rations in their packs,
Rolling their sleeping bags, cleaning their weapons.
He labored with stiff fingers.

                  Trucks drew up.
Outside.

     "Get a move on!" a corporal shouted.

Dodd hitched on his pack.

                The company
Fell in and shuffled, straightening their ranks,
Eyes to the right.

        "Let's go!"

                              Dodd took his place
In the line of olive drab, the overcoats,
Helmets, packs, the gloved hands holding weapons.
The roll was called; he answered to his name.

They marched up to the trucks.

                              "Mount up!"

                                        He climbed
Into the truck, and was packed in. The gate
Clanged shut behind him.


                    X

Day turned to dusk; the truck went jolting on;
The wind was drumming on the canvas hood
And prying coldly down the runner's back.
Dusk turned to evening, and the trucks behind
Were hidden. He dozed off. Monotony
Had numbed his senses like an anesthetic.
When the gears shifted he would nearly wake.
Sometimes the truck would stop for no clear reason,
And faces, blinking in their woolen caps,
Lifted and muttered; someone tried to stretch,
And this set off a ripple of complaints.
Then the truck moved again.
                              Once they dismounted,
And Dodd saw that the road wound through a forest.
There was a hill on one side; on the other,
The trees descended into a ravine.
Against that bank, a group of people stood:
Women and children dressed in country black,
With kerchiefs round their heads, and an old man
Close by a cart. The cart was piled with things:
A mattress, pots and pans. They stood in silence
Watching the soldiers. Then the trucks re-loaded,
And the onlookers vanished.
                              They were driving
More slowly now. The men were all awake.
Another stop. Again the tailgate opened,
And they dismounted.

This, then, was the place.
Colliding in the dark, they formed platoons,
And marched away.

A signpost read *Bastogne*.
They marched through a dark village with locked doors,
And were led off the road, into the woods.
The path was very dark, the march confused,
With frequent halts.

They halted in one place
Endlessly; they reclined, propped on their packs.
His helmet dragged Dodd's head back on his neck;
His feet got cold; under his woolen shirt
The sweat was trickling, then began to chill.

Then they were roused, pressed on without a pause,
Till, on a ridge commanding a black slope,
They halted. And the order came: "Dig in!"

Dodd unhitched his pack, laid it on the ground,
And leaned his rifle on it. From his belt
He took his trench tool out, and opened it.
He stuck the shovel blade into the ground
And levered it. He'd barely circumscribed
A foxhole, when a cold chill touched his cheek—
Snow!

That's all we needed, the runner said
To the malignant sky.

From branch to branch
Snow glimmered down and speckled the dim ground.
Dodd dragged a fallen branch across his hole
And made a roof.

"Pack up," the sergeant said.
"We're moving out."

God help them, they were led
By officers and morons, who had orders
For wearing leather out and breaking spades,
To give employment to the men at home
Who, on this freezing night, were warm in bed
With soldiers' wives!

                    Having said so, they walked
On in the stumbling dark, till once again
They halted, in a place just like the first.

"Dig in!"

                    And it was useless, but they dug
With the energy of a supreme contempt
Marvelous holes—each clammy wedge of earth
An accusation flung in heaven's face.

Then, like a sound engendered by their mood,
An angry muttering rose on the night.
It faded, and again came to their ears—
The sound of guns.

                    At last, Dodd's hole was finished.
He lowered himself, rolled out his sleeping bag,
And pushed into it. Flickerings of light
Twitched overhead; the guns were coming closer.
Here, it was still. The snow came drifting down.

"Dodd, you're on guard."

                    He climbed out of his hole.

"There, by the trees."

                    He walked across the snow,
And as he went he looked around, astonished—
The sky was lit with spots of burning red
In a great circle.

                    As he stood on guard,
Surveying the black slope, the distant fires,
A man approached. Dodd challenged him. He spoke
The password, and came slogging through the trees.
A runner from Battalion. Brushing snow
Out of his neck, he asked for the C. P.
Dodd pointed: "Over there. Close to the barn.
What's happening now?"

                    "We're up a creek, that's what!
They're coming—panzers from the Russians front,
Under Von Runstedt. Panzers and SS.
I was just talking to a man who said

The line at St. Vith has been overrun
By tanks. It was a total massacre.
They're dropping paratroopers too," he said,
And turned away. He paused again to add:
"Everyone else is pulling out but us,"
And trudged away, leaving Dodd to his thoughts.


## XI

The night was long. And day seemed less to rise
Than darkness to withdraw. Dodd, in his hole,
Could hear the fire of small arms, that seems
More threatening to the solitary man
Than does artillery.

                    One hole away
A helmet like a turtle shell was stirring.
A puffy face with whiskers turned around;
It was the mailman, Lopez. He arranged
Twigs on the snow. On these, his drinking mug.
He struck a match, applied it to the twigs,
And nursed the flame with cupped hands, bending over.

Under the hanging sky, congealed with clouds,
Fog trailed and clung to the earth; and the Ardennes,
The spectral firs, their branches cloaked with snow,
Stood stark against the foggy atmosphere.

Dodd stamped his feet. He stooped, and from his pack
Took a K-ration box. He tore it open,
Shook out the can of egg, the pack of biscuits,
The packet of coffee. He removed a glove
And with that hand put snow into his mug.
Poured coffee in, and mixed it with his spoon.
He scooped a hollow in the snow, and piled
Some twigs in it, and strips of the ration box.
And then put the mug on, and lit the pile.

Voices came floating up—loud gutturals;
A whine and clanking of machinery.
He picked his gun up.

                    At the foot of the slope
The trees were shaking, parting. There emerged
A cannon barrel with a muzzle brake.
It slid out like a snake's head, slowly swinging.
It paused. A flash of light came from its head;
A thunder clap exploded to Dodd's left;
Metal whanged on the slope, a spume of black
Hung in the air.

                  Then, endlessly it seemed,
The barrel slid out. With a thrash of branches
A tank appeared. It lurched, seemed to consider,
And then came on, at an appalling rate.
The engine whined; the tracks jingled and squeaked.
And imperceptibly, out of the trees
Stood men, like apparitions of the snow.

And now it was a swarm of walking men
In field-gray and in white, with capes and hoods.

Dodd placed his elbows on the snow, took aim—
There was another thunder clap. He ducked
And came upright again. To left and right
Rifles were firing. Hastily he pointed
The muzzle at a running, hooded shape,
And pressed the trigger. As in a nightmare
Nothing happened. A bullet cracked by his head.
The safety catch was on. He pressed it forward,
And aimed the gun again, and squeezed the trigger.
The butt kicked in his shoulder, the brass jumped
Into the snow.

                  The tank was growing large.
The cannon flashed. Machine-gun tracers curved
Toward it, and played sparkling on the steel.
Still it came on, glittering in return
From its machine guns. Then, a crashing flame
Struck it, leaving a trail of smoke in air.
The tank shuddered. It slewed broadside around.
Inside the plates, as on an anvil, hammers
Were laboring. It trembled with explosions,
And smoke poured out of it.

                         The slope was still,
Sprawling with hooded figures—and the rest
Gone back into the trees. Then there began
The sound of the wounded.

                         Dodd stood up
And looked around. In the next hole, a helmet
Moved cautiously.

                    "Lopez," he inquired,
"Are you all right?"

                         "Jesus!" the mailman said.

With a shaking hand, Dodd felt for cigarettes.
He breathed tobacco deep into his lungs.
On the twigs where he had left it balanced
His mug was hissing and—he held it—warm.


                    XII

Sometimes the snow came drifing down again.
And when it ceased, eddies and gusts of wind
Would lift it in long skirts that swept across
The dead. It packed into the stiffened folds
Of clothing. When night fell, a freezing wind
Encased the tree trunks in bright sheaths of ice
And hung bright icicles on every branch,
And clamped the dead in rigid attitudes.

A shell came whistling down. The runner clenched
His fists. It crashed. Another shell came in.
The crashes jarred the ground. Then, from the rear,
A battery replied; shells fluttered back.

"Dodd!"

          He unzipped his bag, put on his helmet,
And stood.

               "Where are you?"

                         It was the First Sergeant.

"Here," the runner answered.

"Take this message
Back to Battalion. Are you listening?"

"Yes," he said.

"To Colonel Jesserman.
The Captain says we need a fifty-seven
Or tank-destroyer. Tell him that it's urgent.
Now you repeat the message."

Dodd did so.
He slung his rifle over his right shoulder
And climbed out of his hole.

"Keep out of trouble,"
The sergeant said. "Don't stop for anything."
Dodd started to move off. The sergeant grasped
His arm: "Watch out! They may have got patrols
Between us and Battalion. Good luck!"

Dodd waved his hand, although it was too dark
For the other to see him. And set off
In what seemed to be the right direction.

*Rome. December 2, 1957*

# Old Soldier

A dream of battle on a windy night
Has wakened him. The shadows move once more
With rumors of alarm. He sees the height
And helmet of his terror in the door.

The guns reverberate; a livid arc
From sky to sky lightens the windowpanes
And all his room. The clock ticks in the dark;
A cool wind stirs the curtains, and it rains.

He lies remembering: "That's how it was . . ."
And smiles, and drifts into a youthful sleep
Without a care. His life is all he has,
And that is given to the guards to keep.

# The Bird

*"Ich wünscht', ich wäre ein Vöglein,"*
Sang Heinrich, "I would fly
Across the sea . . ." so sadly
It made his mother cry.

At night he played his zither,
By day worked in the mine.
His friend was Hans; together
The boys walked by the Rhine.

"Each day we're growing older,"
Hans said, "This is no life.
I wish I were a soldier!"
And snapped his pocketknife.

War came, and Hans was taken,
But Heinrich did not fight.
*"Ich wünscht', ich wäre ein Vöglein,"*
Sang Heinrich every night.

"Dear Heinrich," said the letter,
"I hope this finds you fine.
The war could not be better,
It's women, song, and wine."

A letter came for Heinrich,
The same that he'd sent East
To Hans, his own handwriting
Returned, and marked *Deceased*.

\*

"You'll never be a beauty,"
The doctor said, "You scamp!
We'll give you special duty—
A concentration camp."

And now the truck was nearing
The place. They passed a house;
A radio was blaring
The *Wiener Blut* of Strauss.

The banks were bright with flowers,
The birds sang in the wood;
There was a fence with towers
On which armed sentries stood.

They stopped. The men dismounted;
Heinrich got down—at last!
"That chimney," said the sergeant,
"That's where the Jews are gassed."

                *

Each day he sorted clothing,
Skirt, trousers, boot, and shoe,
Till he was filled with loathing
For every size of Jew.

"Come in! What is it, Private?"
"Please Sir, that vacancy . . .
I wonder, could I have it?"
"Your papers! Let me see . . .

"You're steady and you're sober . . .
But have you learned to kill?"
Said Heinrich, "No, *Herr Ober-
Leutnant*, but I will!"

"The Reich can use your spirit.
Report to Unit Four.
Here is an armband—wear it!
Dismissed! Don't slam the door."

                *

*"Ich wünscht', ich wäre ein Vöglein,"*
Sang Heinrich, "I would fly . . ."
They knew that when they heard him
The next day they would die.

They stood in silence praying
At midnight when they heard
The zither softly playing,
The singing of the Bird.

He stared into the fire,
He sipped a glass of wine.
*"Ich wünscht'*," his voice rose higher,
*"Ich wäre ein Vöglein . . ."*

A dog howled in its kennel,
He thought of Hans and cried.
The stars looked down from heaven.
That day the children died.

*

"The Russian tanks are coming!"
The wind bore from the East
A cannonade, a drumming
Of small arms that increased.

Heinrich went to Headquarters.
He found the Colonel dead
With pictures of his daughters,
A pistol by his head.

He thought, his courage sinking,
"There's always the SS . . ."
He found the Major drinking
In a woman's party dress.

The prisoners were shaking
Their barracks. Heinrich heard
A sound of timber breaking,
A shout, "Where is the Bird?"

*

The Russian was completing
A seven-page report.
He wrote: "We still are beating
The woods . . ." then he stopped short.

A little bird was flitting
Outside, from tree to tree.
He turned where he was sitting
And watched it thoughtfully.

He pulled himself together,
And wrote: "We've left no stone
Unturned—but not a feather!
It seems the Bird has flown.

"Description? Half a dozen
Group snapshots, badly blurred;
And which is Emma's cousin
God knows, and which the Bird!

"He could be in the Western
Or in the Eastern Zone.
I'd welcome a suggestion
If anything is known."

*

"*Ich wünscht', ich wäre ein Vöglein,*"
Sings Heinrich, "I would fly
Across the sea," so sadly
It makes his children cry.

# The Silent Generation

When Hitler was the Devil
He did as he had sworn
With such enthusiasm
That even, *donnerwetter*,
The Germans say,"Far better
Had he been never born!"

It was my generation
That put the Devil down
With great enthusiasm.
But now our occupation
Is gone. Our education
Is wasted on the town.

We lack enthusiasm.
Life seems a mystery;
It's like the play a lady
Told me about: "It's not . . .
It doesn't *have* a plot,"
She said, "It's history."

# The Lover's Ghost

I fear the headless man
Whose military scars
Proclaim his merit.
And yet I fear a woman
More than the ghost of Mars,
A wounded spirit.

That look, all kindness lost,
Cold hands, as cold as stone,
A wanton gesture—
"What do you want, old ghost?
How long must I atone?"
So I addressed her.

"Did you not call?" she said,
"Goodbye, then! For I go
Where I am wanted."
Till dawn I tossed in bed
Wishing that I could know
Who else she haunted.

# The Goodnight

*He stood still by her bed*
*Watching his daughter breathe,*
*The dark and silver head,*
*The fingers curled beneath,*
*And thought:* Though she may have
Intelligence and charm
And luck, they will not save
Her life from every harm.

The lives of children are
Dangerous to their parents
With fire, water, air,
And other accidents;
And some, for a child's sake,
Anticipating doom,
Empty the world to make
The world safe as a room.

Who could endure the pain
That was Laocoön's?
Twisting, he saw again
In the same coil his sons.
Plumed in his father's skill,
Young Icarus flew higher
Toward the sun, until
He fell in rings of fire.

A man who cannot stand
Children's perilous play,
With lifted voice and hand
Drives the children away.
Out of sight, out of reach,
The tumbling children pass;
He sits on an empty beach,
Holding an empty glass.

Who said that tenderness
Will turn the heart to stone?
May I endure her weakness

As I endure my own.
Better to say goodnight
To breathing flesh and blood
Each night as though the night
Were always only good.

# At the End
## of the Open Road
## 1963

# In California

Here I am, troubling the dream coast
With my New York face,
Bearing among the realtors
And tennis players my dark preoccupation.

There once was an epical clatter—
Voices and banjos, Tennessee, Ohio,
Rising like incense in the sight of heaven.
Today, there is an angel in the gate.

Lie back, Walt Whitman,
There, on the fabulous raft with the King and the Duke!
For the white row of the Marina
Faces the Rock. Turn round the wagons here.

Lie back! We cannot bear
The stars any more, those infinite spaces.
Let the realtors divide the mountain,
For they have already subdivided the valley.

Rectangular city blocks astonished
Herodotus in Babylon,
Cortez in Tenochtitlan,
And here's the same old city-planner, death.

We cannot turn or stay.
For though we sleep, and let the reins fall slack,
The great cloud-wagons move
Outward still, dreaming of a Pacific.

# In the Suburbs

There's no way out.
You were born to waste your life.
You were born to this middleclass life

As others before you
Were born to walk in procession
To the temple, singing.

# The Redwoods

Mountains are moving, rivers
are hurrying. But we
are still.

We have the thoughts of giants—
clouds, and at night the stars.

And we have names—guttural, grotesque—
Hamet, Og—names with no syllables.

And perish, one by one, our roots
gnawed by the mice. And fall.

And are too slow for death, and change
to stone. Or else too quick,

like candles in a fire. Giants
are lonely. We have waited long

for someone. By our waiting, surely
there must be someone at whose touch

our boughs would bend; and hands
to gather us; a spirit

to whom we are light as the hawthorn tree.
O if there is a poet

let him come now! We stand at the Pacific
like great unmarried girls,

turning in our heads the stars and clouds,
considering whom to please.

# There Is

Look! From my window there's a view
of city streets
where only lives as dry as tortoises
can crawl—the Gallapagos of desire.

There is the day of Negroes with red hair
and the day of insane women on the subway;
there is the day of the word Trieste
and the night of the blind man with the electric guitar.

But I have no profession. Like a spy
I read the papers—Situations Wanted.
Surely there is a secret
which, if I knew it, would change everything!

2

I have the poor man's nerve-tic, irony.
I see through the illusions of the age!
The bell tolls, and the hearse advances,
and the mourners follow, for my entertainment.

I tread the burning pavement,
the streets where drunkards stretch
like photographs of civil death
and trumpets strangle in electric shelves.

The mannequins stare at me scornfully.
I know they are pretending
all day to be in earnest.
And can it be that love is an illusion?

When darkness falls on the enormous street
the air is filled with Eros, whispering.
Eyes, mouths, contrive to meet
in silence, fearing they may be prevented.

3

O businessmen like ruins,
bankers who are Bastilles,
widows, sadder than the shores of lakes,
then you were happy, when you still could tremble!

But all night long my window
sheds tears of light.
I seek the word. The word is not forthcoming.
O syllables of light . . . O dark cathedral . . .

# Summer Morning

There are whole blocks in New York
Where no one lives—
A district of small factories.
And there's a hotel; one morning

When I was there with a girl
We saw in the window opposite
Men and women working at their machines.
Now and then one looked up.

Toys, hardware—whatever they made,
It's been worn out.
I'm fifteen years older myself—
Bad years and good.

So I have spoiled my chances.
For what? Sheer laziness,
The thrill of an assignation,
My life that I hold in secret.

# Birch

Birch tree, you remind me
Of a room filled with breathing,
The sway and whisper of love.

She slips off her shoes;
Unzips her skirt; arms raised,
Unclasps an earring, and the other.

Just so the sallow trunk
Divides, and the branches
Are pale and smooth.

# The Morning Light

In the morning light a line
Stretches forever. There my unlived life
Rises, and I resist,
Clinging to the steps of the throne.

Day lifts the darkness from the hills,
A bright blade cuts the reeds,
And my life, pitilessly demanding,
Rises forever in the morning light.

# The Cradle Trap

A bell and rattle,
a smell of roses,
a leather Bible,
and angry voices . . .

They say, I love you.
They shout, You must!
The light is telling
terrible stories.

But night at the window
whispers, Never mind.
Be true, be true
to your own strange kind.

# A Story About Chicken Soup

In my grandmother's house there was always chicken soup
And talk of the old country—mud and boards,
Poverty,
The snow falling down the necks of lovers.

Now and then, out of her savings
She sent them a dowry. Imagine
The rice-powdered faces!
And the smell of the bride, like chicken soup.

But the Germans killed them.
I know it's in bad taste to say it,
But it's true. The Germans killed them all.

*

In the ruins of Berchtesgaden
A child with yellow hair
Ran out of a doorway.

A German girl-child—
Cuckoo, all skin and bones—
Not even enough to make chicken soup.
She sat by the stream and smiled.

Then as we splashed in the sun
She laughed at us.
We had killed her mechanical brothers,
So we forgave her.

*

The sun is shining.
The shadows of the lovers have disappeared.
They are all eyes; they have some demand on me—
They want me to be more serious than I want to be.

They want me to stick in their mudhole
Where no one is elegant.
They want me to wear old clothes,
They want me to be poor, to sleep in a room with many others—

Not to walk in the painted sunshine
To a summer house,
But to live in the tragic world forever.

# The Troika

Troika, troika! The snow moon
whirls through the forest.

Where lamplight like a knife
gleams through a door, I see two graybeards bending.
They're playing chess, it seems. And then one rises
and stands in silence. Does he hear me passing?

Troika, troika! In the moonlight
his spirit hears my spirit passing.

I whip the horses on. The houses vanish.
The moon looks over fields
littered with debris. And there in trenches
the guardsmen stand, wind fluttering their rags.

And there were darker fields without a moon.
I walk across a field, bound on an errand.
The errand's forgotten—something depended on it.
A nightmare! I have lost my father's horses!

And then a white bird rises
and goes before me, hopping through the forest.

I held the bird—it vanished with a cry,
and on a branch a girl sat sideways, combing
her long black hair. The dew
shone on her lips; her breasts were white as roses.

Troika, troika! Three white horses,
a whip of silver, and my father's sleigh . . .

When morning breaks, the sea
gleams through the branches,
and the white bird, enchanted,
is flying through the world, across the sea.

# New Lines for Cuscuscaraway and Mirza Murad Ali Beg

*. . . the particular verse we are going to get will be cheerful, dry and sophisticated.*

T. E. HULME

O amiable prospect!
O kingdom of heaven on earth!
I saw Mr. Eliot leaning over a fence
Like a cheerful embalmer,
And two little Indians with black umbrellas
Seeking admission,
And I was rapt in a song
Of so*phist*ication.
O City of God!
Let us be thoroughly dry.
Let us sing a new song unto the Lord,
A song of exclusion.
For it is not so much a matter of being chosen
As of not being excluded.
I will sing unto the Lord
In a voice that is cheerfully dry.

# Moving the Walls

The Prince of Monaco
Was sick of English ladies.

The Prince had a yacht
And her name was *Hirondelle*.
She was cousin to the yacht of the Kaiser
And niece to the yacht of the Tsar.

And the Prince was interested in the sea—
That is, oceanography.
So he furnished the yacht with instruments
And with instruments of brass,
Burners and sinks and instruments
Of the most delicate glass.

There was also a whaleboat
And a whole crew of harpooners.
There was a helmet and suit of armor
For the wars of the ocean floor.

The *Hirondelle* trembled like a fern,
And the crew stood at attention,
And they piped the Captain aboard.


2


Cloud-sailed, the *Hirondelle*
Pursued the horizon.
At night she skimmed
The phosphorescent surges.

And now they are on the Pacific,
The bottomless sea.
And out of the deep they have drawn
The whale, Leviathan, with a hook.
They have captured the giant squid
That has ten arms, claws like a cat's, a beak like a parrot's,
And a large malevolent eye.

They stepped from the whaleboat onto shoals,
The crests of sunken mountains.

In nets they gathered
Plankton and weeds and crabs that looked astonished.

And there were nights, O Prince,
When you stretched your hands and feet
In the leaves of the pomegranate tree!

And all went into the log.
The various sea trophies
Were written down in the log.
The darkening sky, the storm,
And tranquil days—
All, all went into the log.


### 3

The Prince returned—a hero of sorts.
He returned to his former life,
To the lights of the Grand Hotel
And the Russian ladies with their eternal cigarettes.

Then he built a museum.
The wheel of the *Hirondelle* is there,
And also the laboratory, the strange heart of the ship
Uprooted, leaving red holes
In the deck that vanished in smoke.

Here are the trophies:
A walking stick made from the backbone of a shark;
Tortoiseshell combs, and fans of mother-of-pearl;
Corals that faded,
Losing the changing hues of sea and sky;
Sea shells under glass
That are as dull as buttons
Sewn on garments by girls who have faded.

The Philippine Islands are a box
And the smile of a lady in a mantilla.

A walrus stuffed with straw
Faces the diving helmet.
They remember Verdun and Passchendaele,
The mud-clouded wars of the ocean floor.

So all that oceanography, after all,
Was only a pawnshop.
For they brought home the tooth of the whale
And said, "Look!
It is only a doorstop, after all."

For Leviathan does not exist,
And the sea is no mystery.
For a shark is a walking stick.

And this we call the life of reason.


4

Idiots!
We too are all for reducing
The universe to human dimensions.
As if we could know what is human!

Just a few dippers of sea water
And a fair wind home . . .
Then surely we won't be destroyed.

A strange idea, if you consider
The dust of those settlements—
The parlors where no one lives;
The splinter that wounds the foot-sole
On its way to the double bed;
And Leviathan over all,
The cloud shaped like a weasel or a whale,
Leviathan rising above the roof tops.


5

When men wanted the golden fleece
It was not wool they wanted.
*They* were the trophies that they sailed toward.

They were the sea and the wind
That hurled them over
Into the sea. They were the fishes
That stripped their thin bones. And they rose
In the night in new constellations.

They left no wreckage.
Nothing is floating on the surface.
For they yielded themselves
To the currents that moved from within.

They are mightily changed
In the corollas, the branched sea-heaven.

And you, my country,
These days your walls are moving,
These nights we are branching among the stars.

I say, but my mind is doubtful.
Are there any at sea?
If so, they have not whispered lately.

# Frogs

The storm broke, and it rained,
And water rose in the pool,
And frogs hopped into the gutter,

With their skins of yellow and green,
And just their eyes shining above the surface
Of the warm solution of slime.

At night, when fireflies trace
Light-lines between the trees and flowers
Exhaling perfume,

The frogs speak to each other
In rhythm. The sound is monstrous,
But their voices are filled with satisfaction.

In the city I pine for the country;
In the country I long for conversation—
Our happy croaking.

# My Father in the Night Commanding No

My father in the night commanding No
Has work to do. Smoke issues from his lips;
    He reads in silence.
The frogs are croaking and the street lamps glow.

And then my mother winds the gramophone;
The Bride of Lammermoor begins to shriek—
    Or reads a story
About a prince, a castle, and a dragon.

The moon is glittering above the hill.
I stand before the gateposts of the King—
    So runs the story—
Of Thule, at midnight when the mice are still.

And I have been in Thule! It has come true—
The journey and the danger of the world,
    All that there is
To bear and to enjoy, endure and do.

Landscapes, seascapes . . . where have I been led?
The names of cities—Paris, Venice, Rome—
    Held out their arms.
A feathered god, seductive, went ahead.

Here is my house. Under a red rose tree
A child is swinging; another gravely plays.
    They are not surprised
That I am here; they were expecting me.

And yet my father sits and reads in silence,
My mother sheds a tear, the moon is still,
    And the dark wind
Is murmuring that nothing ever happens.

Beyond his jurisdiction as I move
Do I not prove him wrong? And yet, it's true
    *They* will not change
There, on the stage of terror and of love.

The actors in that playhouse always sit
In fixed positions—father, mother, child

With painted eyes.
How sad it is to be a little puppet!

Their heads are wooden. And you once pretended
To understand them! Shake them as you will,
        They cannot speak.
Do what you will, the comedy is ended.

Father, why did you work? Why did you weep,
Mother? Was the story so important?
        *"Listen!"* the wind
Said to the children, and they fell asleep.

# American Poetry

Whatever it is, it must have
A stomach that can digest
Rubber, coal, uranium, moons, poems.

Like the shark, it contains a shoe.
It must swim for miles through the desert
Uttering cries that are almost human.

# The Inner Part

When they had won the war
And for the first time in history
Americans were the most important people—

When the leading citizens no longer lived in their shirt sleeves,
And their wives did not scratch in public;
Just when they'd stopped saying "Gosh!"—

When their daughters seemed as sensitive
As the tip of a fly rod,
And their sons were as smooth as a V–8 engine—

Priests, examining the entrails of birds,
Found the heart misplaced, and seeds
As black as death, emitting a strange odor.

# On the Lawn at the Villa

On the lawn at the villa—
That's the way to start, eh, reader?
We know where we stand—somewhere expensive—
You and I *imperturbes*, as Walt would say,
Before the diversions of wealth, you and I *engagés*.

On the lawn at the villa
Sat a manufacturer of explosives,
His wife from Paris,
And a young man named Bruno,

And myself, being American,
Willing to talk to these malefactors,
The manufacturer of explosives, and so on,
But somehow superior. By that I mean democratic.
It's complicated, being an American,
Having the money and the bad conscience, both at the same time.
Perhaps, after all, this is not the right subject for a poem.

We were all sitting there paralyzed
In the hot Tuscan afternoon,
And the bodies of the machine-gun crew were draped over the
    balcony.
So we sat there all afternoon.

# The Riders Held Back

One morning, as we travelled in the fields
    Of air and dew
With trumpets, and above the painted shields
    The banners flew,

We came upon three ladies, wreathed in roses,
    Where, hand in hand,
They danced—three slender, gentle, naked ladies,
    All in a woodland.

They'd been to the best schools in Italy;
    Their legs were Greek,
Their collarbones, as fine as jewelry,
    Their eyes, antique.

"Why do lambs skip and shepherds shout 'Ut hoy!'?
    Why do you dance?"
Said one, "It is an intellectual joy,
    The Renaissance.

"As do the stars in heaven, ruled by Three,
    We twine and move.
It is the music of Astronomy,
    Not men, we love.

"And as we dance, the beasts and flowers do;
    The fields of wheat
Sway like our arms; the curving hills continue
    The curves of our feet.

"Here Raphael comes to paint; the thrushes flute
    To Petrarch's pen.
But Michael is not here, who carved the brute
    Unfinished men."

They danced again, and on the mountain heights
    There seemed to rise
Towers and ramparts glittering with lights,
    Like Paradise.

How the bright morning passed, I cannot say.
    We woke and found
The dancers gone; and heard, far, far away
    The trumpet sound.

We galloped to it. In the forest then
    Banners and shields
Were strewn like leaves; and there were many slain
    In the dark fields.

# A Farm in Minnesota

The corn rows walk the earth,
crowding like mankind between the fences,
feeding on sun and rain;
are broken down by hail,
or perish of incalculable drought.

And we who tend them
from the ground up—lieutenants
of this foot cavalry, leaning on fences
to watch our green men never move an inch—
who cares for us?

Our beds are sold at auction.
The Bible, and a sword—these are bequeathed
to children who prefer a modern house.
Our flesh has been consumed
only to make more lives.

But when our heads are planted
under the church, from those empty pods
we rise in the fields of death,
and are gathered by angels,
and shine in the hands of God.

# Love, My Machine

Love, my machine,
We rise by this escape,
We travel on the shocks we make.

For every man and woman
Is an immortal spirit
Trapped and dazed on a star shoot.

Tokyo, come in!
Yuzuru Karagiri, do you read me?
San Francisco, darkest of cities, do you read me?

Here is eternal space,
Here is eternal solitude.
Is it any different with you on earth?

There are so many here!
Here's Gandhi, here's Jesus,
Moses, and all the other practical people.

By the light of the stars
This night is serious.
I am going into the night to find a world of my own.

# Wind, Clouds, and the Delicate Curve of the World

Wind, clouds, and the delicate curve of the world
Stretching so far away . . .
On a cloud in the clear sight of heaven
Sit Kali and Jesus, disputing.
Tree shadows, cloud shadows
Falling across the body of the world
That sleeps with one arm thrown across her eyes . . .
A wind stirs in the daisies
And trees are sighing,
"These houses and these gardens are illusions."
Leaf shadows, cloud shadows,
And the wind moving as far as the eye can reach . . .

# Walt Whitman at Bear Mountain

*. . . life which does not give the preference to any other life, of any previous period, which therefore prefers its own existence . . .*

ORTEGA Y GASSET

Neither on horesback nor seated,
But like himself, squarely on two feet,
The poet of death and lilacs
Loafs by the footpath. Even the bronze looks alive
Where it is folded like cloth. And he seems friendly.

"Where is the Mississippi panorama
And the girl who played the piano?
Where are you, Walt?
The Open Road goes to the used-car lot.

"Where is the nation you promised?
These houses built of wood sustain
Colossal snows,
And the light above the street is sick to death.

"As for the people—see how they neglect you!
Only a poet pauses to read the inscription."

"I am here," he answered.
"It seems you have found me out.
Yet, did I not warn you that it was Myself
I advertised? Were my words not sufficiently plain?

"I gave no prescriptions,
And those who have taken my moods for prophecies
Mistake the matter."
Then, vastly amused—"Why do you reproach me?
I freely confess I am wholly disreputable.
Yet I am happy, because you have found me out."

A crocodile in wrinkled metal loafing . . .

Then all the realtors,
Pickpockets, salesmen, and the actors performing
Official scenarios,

Turned a deaf ear, for they had contracted
American dreams.

But the man who keeps a store on a lonely road,
And the housewife who knows she's dumb,
And the earth, are relieved.

All that grave weight of America
Cancelled! Like Greece and Rome.
The future in ruins!
The castles, the prisons, the cathedrals
Unbuilding, and roses
Blossoming from the stones that are not there . . .

The clouds are lifting from the high Sierras,
The Bay mists clearing.
And the angel in the gate, the flowering plum,
Dances like Italy, imagining red.

# Pacific Ideas—A Letter to Walt Whitman

When the schooners were drifting
Over the hills—schooners like white skulls—
The sun was the clock in that parlor
And the piano was played by the wind.

But a man must sit down,
And things, after all, are necessary.
Those "immensely overpaid accounts,"
Walt, it seems that we must pay them again.

It's hard to civilize, to change
The usual order;
And the young, who are always the same, endlessly
Rehearse the fate of Achilles.

Everyone wants to live at the center,
"The world of the upper floors."
And the sad professors of English
Are wishing that they were dead, as usual.

But here is the sea and the mist,
Gray Lethe of forgetfulness,
And the moon, gliding from the mist,
Love, with her garland of dreams.

And I have quarrelled with my books
For the moon is not in their fable,
And say to darkness, Let your dragon come,
O anything, to hold her in my arms!

# Lines Written Near San Francisco

I wake and feel the city trembling.
Yes, there is something unsettled in the air
And the earth is uncertain.

And so it was for the tenor Caruso.
He couldn't sleep—you know how the ovation
Rings in your ears, and you re-sing your part.

And then the ceiling trembled
And the floor moved. He ran into the street.
Never had Naples given him such a reception!

The air was darker than Vesuvius.
"*O mamma mia*,"
He cried, "I've lost my voice!"

At that moment the hideous voice of Culture,
Hysterical woman, thrashing her arms and legs,
Shrieked from the ruins.

At that moment everyone became a performer.
Otello and Don Giovanni
And Figaro strode on the midmost stage.

In the high window of a burning castle
Lucia raved. Black horses
Plunged through fire, dragging the wild bells.

The curtains were wrapped in smoke. Tin swords
Were melting; masks and ruffs
Burned—and the costumes of the peasants' chorus.

Night fell. The white moon rose
And sank in the Pacific. The tremors
Passed under the waves. And Death rested.


2

Now, as we stand idle,
Watching the silent, bowler-hatted man,
The engineer, who writes in the smoking field;

Now as he hands the paper to a boy,
Who takes it and runs to a group of waiting men,
And they disperse and move toward their wagons,

Mules bray and the wagons move—
Wait! Before you start
(Already the wheels are rattling on the stones)

Say, did your fathers cross the dry Sierras
To build another London?
Do Americans always have to be second-rate?

Wait! For there are spirits
In the earth itself, or the air, or sea.
Where are the aboriginal American devils?

Cloud shadows, pine shadows
Falling across the bright Pacific bay . . .
(Already they have nailed rough boards together)

Wait only for the wind
That rustles in the eucalyptus tree.
Wait only for the light

That trembles on the petals of a rose.
(The mortar sets—banks are the first to stand)
Wait for a rose, and you may wait forever.

The silent man mops his head and drinks
Cold lemonade. "San Francisco
Is a city second only to Paris."


3

Every night, at the end of America
We taste our wine, looking at the Pacific.
How sad it is, the end of America!

While we were waiting for the land
They'd finished it—with gas drums
On the hilltops, cheap housing in the valleys

Where lives are mean and wretched.
But the banks thrive and the realtors
Rejoice—they have their America.

Still, there is something unsettled in the air.
Out there on the Pacific
There's no America but the Marines.

Whitman was wrong about the People,
But right about himself. The land is within.
At the end of the open road we come to ourselves.

Though mad Columbus follows the sun
Into the sea, we cannot follow.
We must remain, to serve the returning sun,

And to set tables for death.
For we are the colonists of Death—
Not, as some think, of the English.

And we are preparing thrones for him to sit,
Poems to read, and beds
In which it may please him to rest.

This is the land
The pioneers looked for, shading their eyes
Against the sun—a murmur of serious life.

# Selected Poems
## 1965

# The Union Barge on Staten Island

The crazy pier, a roof of splinters
Stretched over the sea,
Was a cattle barge. It sailed in the Civil War,
In the time of the Wilderness battles.
The beams are charred, the deck worn soft between the knotholes.

When the barge sank offshore
They drove the cattle on land and slaughtered them here.
What tasty titbits that day
For the great squawking seagulls and pipers!
A hooded shuffling over the dark sand . . .

Under your feet, the wood seems deeply alive.
It's the running sea you feel.
Those animals felt the same currents,
And the drifting clouds
Are drifting over the Wilderness, over the still farms.

# Columbus

*To find the Western path,*
*Right thro' the Gates of Wrath . . .*
                                    BLAKE

As I walked with my friend,
My singular Columbus,
Where the land comes to an end
And the path is perilous,
Where the wheel and tattered shoe
And bottle have been thrown,
And the sky is shining blue,
And the heart sinks like a stone,

I plucked his sleeve and said,
"I have come far to find
The springs of a broken bed,
The ocean, and the wind.
I'd rather live in Greece,
Castile, or an English town
Than wander here like this
Where the dunes come tumbling down."

He answered me, "Perhaps.
But Europe never guessed
America, their maps
Could not describe the West.
And though in Plato's glass
The stars were still and clear,
Yet nothing came to pass
And men died of despair."

He said, "If there is not
A way to China, one
City surpassing thought,
My ghost will still go on.
I'll spread the airy sail,"
He said, "and point the sprit
To a country that cannot fail,
For there's no finding it."

Straightway we separated—
He, in his fading coat,
To the water's edge, where waited
An admiral's longboat.
A crew of able seamen
Sprang up at his command—
An angel or a demon—
And they rowed him from the land.

# The Laurel Tree

In the clear light that confuses everything
Only you, dark laurel,
Shadow my house,

Lifting your arms in the anguish
Of nature at the stake.
And at night, quivering with tears,

You are like the tree called Tasso's.
Crippled, and hooped with iron,
It stands on Peter's hill.

When the lovers prop their bicycles
And sit on the high benches
That look across to eternity,

That tree makes their own torsion
Seem natural. And so, they're comforted.

2

One of the local philosophers . . .
He says, "In California
We have the old anarchist tradition."

What can he mean? Is there an anarchist tradition?
And why would an anarchist want one?
O California,

Is there a tree without opinions?
Come, let me clasp you!
Let me feel the idea breathing.

I too cry O for a life of sensations
Rather than thoughts—
"The sayling Pine, the Cedar proud and tall."

Like the girls in our neighborhood,
They're beautiful and silent.

### 3

As I was digging in the back yard
I thought of a man in China.
A lifetime, it seemed, we gazed at each other.

I could see and hear his heartbeats
Like a spade hurling clods.
He pointed behind him, and I saw

That the hills were covered with armed men,
And they were all on the other side
Of the life that I held dear.

He said, "We are as various
As the twigs of a tree,
But now the tree moves as one man.

It walks. And the earth trembles
When a race of slaves is leaving."

### 4

I said, "Yet, all these people
Will fall down as one man
When the entrails of a bomb are breathing.

When we came down from Chosin
Carrying the guns in dainty snow-wear
And all the dead we had to,

It was a time of forgetfulness,
Like a plucked string.
It was a river of darkness.

Was it not so on your side, when you came
To the sea that was covered with ships?
Let us speak to each other,

Let the word rise, making dark strokes in the air.
That bird flies over the heads of the armed men."

One part of the tree grows outward.
The other I saw when, with a light,
I explored the cellar—shattering roots.

They had broken through the wall,
As though there were something in my rubbish
That life would have at last.

I must be patient with shapes
Of automobile fenders and ketchup bottles.
These things are the beginning

Of things not visible to the naked eye.
It was so in the time of Tobit—
The dish glowed when the angel held it.

It is so that spiritual messengers
Deliver their meaning.

# Things

A man stood in the laurel tree
Adjusting his hands and feet to the boughs.
He said, "Today I was breaking stones
On a mountain road in Asia,

When suddenly I had a vision
Of mankind, like grass and flowers,
The same over all the earth.
We forgave each other; we gave ourselves
Wholly over to words.
And straightway I was released
And sprang through an open gate."

I said, "Into a meadow?"

He said, "I am impervious to irony.
I thank you for the word. . . .
I am standing in a sunlit meadow.
Know that everything your senses reject
Springs up in the spiritual world."

I said, "Our scientists have another opinion.
They say, you are merely phenomena."

He said, "Over here they will be angels
Singing, Holy holy be His Name!
And also, it works in reverse.
Things which to us in the pure state are mysterious,
Are your simplest articles of household use—
A chair, a dish, and meaner even than these,
The very latest inventions.
Machines are the animals of the Americans—
Tell me about machines."

I said, "I have suspected
The Mixmaster knows more than I do,
The air conditioner is the better poet.
My right front tire is as bald as Odysseus—
How much it must have suffered!

Then, as things have a third substance
Which is obscure to both our senses,
Let there be a perpetual coming and going
Between your house and mine."

# Outward

The staff slips from the hand
Hissing and swims on the polished floor.
It glides away to the desert.

It floats like a bird or lily
On the waves, to the ones who are arriving.
And if no god arrives,

Then everything yearns outward.
The honeycomb cell brims over
And the atom is broken in light.

Machines have made their god. They walk or fly.
The towers bend like Magi, mountains weep,
Needles go mad, and metal sheds a tear.

$$*$$

The astronaut is lifted
Away from the world, and drifts.
How easy it is to be there!

How easy to be anyone, anything but oneself!
The metal of the plane is breathing;
Sinuously it swims through the stars.

# Stumpfoot on 42nd Street

A Negro sprouts from the pavement like an asparagus.
One hand beats a drum and cymbal;
He plays a trumpet with the other.

He flies the American flag;
When he goes walking, from stump to stump,
It twitches, and swoops, and flaps.

Also, he has a tin cup which he rattles;
He shoves it right in your face.
These freaks are alive in earnest.

He is not embarrassed.
It is for you to feel embarrassed,
Or God, or the way things are.

Therefore he plays the trumpet
And therefore he beats the drum.


### 2

I can see myself in Venezuela,
With flowers, and clouds in the distance.
The mind tends to drift.

But Stumpfoot stands near a window
Advertising cameras, trusses, household utensils.
The billboards twinkle. The time
Is 12:26.

O why don't angels speak in the infinite
To each other? Why this confusion,
These particular bodies—
Eros with clenched fists, sobbing and cursing?

The time is 12:26.
The streets lead on in burning lines
And giants tremble in electric chains.

## 3

I can see myself in the middle of Venezuela
Stepping in a nest of ants.
I can see myself being eaten by ants.

My ribs are caught in a thorn bush
And thought has no reality.
But he has furnished his room

With a chair and table.
A chair is like a dog, it waits for man.
He unstraps his apparatus,

And now he is taking off his boots.
He is easing his stumps,
And now he is lighting a cigar.

It seems that a man exists
Only to say, Here I am in person.

# After Midnight

The dark streets are deserted,
With only a drugstore glowing
Softly, like a sleeping body;

With one white, naked bulb
In the back, that shines
On suicides and abortions.

Who lives in these dark houses?
I am suddenly aware
I might live here myself.

The garage man returns
And puts the change in my hand,
Counting the singles carefully.

# Luminous Night

I love the dark race of poets,
And yet there is also happiness.
Happiness . . .

If I can stand it, I can stand anything.
Luminous night, let fall your pearls!
Wind, toss the sodden boughs!

Then let the birch trees shine
Like crystal. Light the boughs!
We can live here, Cristina,

We can live here,
In this house, among these trees,
This world so many have left.

# *Adventures*
## *of the Letter I*
## 1971

# Dvonya

In the town of Odessa
there is a garden
and Dvonya is there,
Dvonya whom I love
though I have never been in Odessa.

I love her black hair, and eyes
as green as a salad
that you gather in August
between the roots of alder,
her skin with an odor of wildflowers.

We understand each other perfectly.
We are cousins twice removed.
In the garden we drink our tea,
discussing the plays of Chekhov
as evening falls and the lights begin to twinkle.

But this is only a dream.
I am not there
with my citified speech,
and the old woman is not there
peering between the curtains.

We are only phantoms, bits of ash,
like yesterday's newspaper
or the smoke of chimneys.
All that passed long ago
on a summer night in Odessa.

# A Son of the Romanovs

This is Avram the cello-mender,
the only Jewish sergeant
in the army of the Tsar.
One day he was mending cellos
when they shouted, "The Tsar is coming,
everyone out for inspection!"
When the Tsar saw Avram marching
with Russians who were seven feet tall,
he said, "He must be a genius.
I want that fellow at headquarters."

Luck is given by God.
A wife you must find for yourself.

So Avram married a rich widow
who lived in a house in Odessa.
The place was filled with music . . .
Yasnaya Polyana with noodles.

One night in the middle of a concert
they heard a knock at the door.
So Avram went. It was a beggar,
a Russian, who had been blessed
by God—that is, he was crazy.
And he said, "I'm a natural son
of the Grand Duke Nicholas."

And Avram said, "Eat.
I owe your people a favor."
And he said, "My wife is complaining
we need someone to open the door."
So Nicholas stayed with them for years.
Who ever heard of Jewish people
with a footman?

And then the Germans came. Imagine
the scene—the old people
holding on to their baggage,
and the children—they've been told it's a game,
but they don't believe it.

Then the German says, "Who's this?"
pointing at Nicholas,
"he doesn't look like a Jew."
And he said, "I'm the natural son
of the Grand Duke Nicholas."
And they saw he was feeble-minded,
and took him away too, to the death-chamber.

"He could have kept his mouth shut,"
said my Grandmother,
"but what can you expect.
All of those Romanovs were a little bit crazy."

# Meyer

In Russia there were three students,
Chaim, Baruch, and Meyer.
"As Maimonides says," said Meyer.
"Speaking of the Flood," said Baruch.
*"Etsev,"* said Chaim, "an equivocal term."

In Spring when the birch trees shine like crystal
and the light is so clear that a butterfly
makes dark strokes in the air,
there came three students of Hebrew
and the girls from the button factory—

Dvoira, Malka, Rifkele . . .
a mystery, a fragrance,
and a torment to the scholars.
They couldn't have kept a goat, for the milk,
much less the fastidious girls of our province.

*

One night, the red star rising,
a beautiful dream came to Meyer,
a *moujik* who gave him a kiss,
and he heard a voice say, "Meyer,
and Lermontov, and Pushkin."

Dark roofs of Volhynia,
do you remember Meyer
who went to the University
and later he joined the Communist Party?
Last night I dreamed of Meyer. . . .

He turned his head and smiled.
With his hand he made a sign . . .
then his features changed, he was mournful,
and I heard him say in a clear voice,
"Beware! These men killed Meyer."

# The Country House

You always know what to expect
in a novel by L. V. Kalinin. . . .

"One morning in June, in the provincial town
of X, had you been observant,
you might have seen a stranger
alighting at the railroad station."

From there it moves to a country house,
introduction of the principal characters—
a beautiful girl, a youth
on fire with radical ideas.

There are drawing-room discussions,
picnics at the lake, or a mountain,
if there is one in the vicinity.

Then some misunderstanding—
the young man banished from the house
by the angry father. Tears.

All this with the most meticulous attention
to the "spirit of the times,"
bearing in mind the classical saying,
"Don't be the first to try anything, or the last."

        \*

The tone of his letters was quite different:

"The Polish girl I told you about, who is living with us,
has a wart. Two days ago, the idiot
tried to remove it with lye.
For hours on end the house has been filled with howling,
and I can't think or write."

# A Night in Odessa

Grandfather puts down his tea glass
and makes his excuses
and sets off, taking his umbrella.
The street lamps shine through a fog
and drunkards reel on the pavement.

One man clenches his fists in anger,
another utters terrible sobs. . . .
And women look on calmly.
They like those passionate sounds.
He walks on, grasping his umbrella.

His path lies near the forest.
Suddenly a wolf leaps in the path,
jaws dripping. The man strikes
with the point of his umbrella. . . .
A howl, and the wolf has vanished.

Go on, grandfather, hop!
It takes brains to live here,
not to be beaten and torn
or to lie drunk in a ditch.
Hold on to your umbrella!

He's home. When he opens the door
his wife jumps up to greet him.
Her name is Ninotchka,
she is young and dark and slender,
married only a month or so.

She hurries to get his supper.
But when she puts down the dish
she presses a hand to her side
and he sees that from her hand
red drops of blood are falling.

# Isidor

Isidor was always plotting
to overthrow the government.
The family lived in one room. . . .
A window rattles,
a woman coughs,
snow drifts over the rooftops . . .
despair. An intelligent household.

One day, there's a knock at the door. . . .
The police! A confusion . . .
Isidor's wife throws herself
on the mattress . . . she groans
as though she is in labor.
The police search everywhere,
and leave. Then a leg comes out . . .
an arm . . . then a head with spectacles.
Isidor was under the mattress!

When I think about my family
I have a feeling of suffocation.
Next time . . . how about the oven?

The mourners are sitting around
weeping and tearing their clothes.
The inspector comes. He looks in the oven . . .
there's Isidor, with his eyes
shut fast . . . his hands are folded.
The inspector nods, and goes.
Then a leg comes out, and the other.
Isidor leaps, he dances . . .

"Praise God, may His Name be exalted!"

# Adam Yankev

Memory rising in the steppes
flows down. On the banks are trees
and towns with golden cupolas.

I can see my mother's family
sitting around the kitchen stove
arguing—the famous Russian theater.

The sisters return—they're breathless,
they've been down to the river—
their arms filled with wildflowers.


## 2

Every Friday I used to go to Brooklyn.
Behold the children of Israel
at the end of the Diaspora!

Old men with beards and *yarmelkehs*,
old women sitting on the benches . . .
Israel, is it you?

Talking about their lives in the Old Country . . .
The passing headlights hurl
their shadows against the wall.


## 3

Though I walk with a head full of ancient life
it's not that life I see, but houses,
streets, bridges, traffic, crowds, a continual

outpouring of phenomena—
the traffic moving along Broadway,
red glow of the theater district.

I feel I am part of a race
that has not yet arrived in America.
Yet, these people—their faces are strangely familiar.

## 4

The first clear star comes gliding
over the trees and dark rooftops,
the same world passing here—

voices and shadows of desire,
and the tears of things. . . . Around us
things want to be understood.

And the moon, so softly gleaming
in furs,
that put a hole through Pushkin.

# Indian Country

### 1. *The Shadow-Hunter*

This prairie light . . . I see
a warrior and a child.

The man points, and the child
runs after a butterfly.

Rising and floating in the windy field,
that's how they learned to run . . .

Plenty Coups,
Red Cloud, Coyote, Pine Marten.

Now I will lie down in the grass
that Plenty Coups loved.

There are voices in the wind, strong voices
in the tenderness of these leaves,

and the deer move with the shade
into the hills I dream of.

There the young men live by hunting
the shadows of ideas,

and at night they march no further.
Their tents shine in the moonlight.

### 2. *Black Kettle Raises the Stars and Stripes*

"Nits make lice," said Chivington.
"Kill the nits and you'll get no lice."

The white men burst in at sunrise, shooting and stabbing.
And there was old Black Kettle
tying the Stars and Stripes to his tent pole,
and the squaws running in every direction

around Sand Creek,
a swept corner of the American consciousness.

And it's no use playing the tuba to a dead Indian.

### 3. *On the Prairie*

The wind in the leaves makes a sound
like clear running water.

I can smell the store where harness used to be sold. . . .
Morning of little leaves,

morning of cool, clear sunlight,
when the house stirred with the earnestness

of the life they really had . . .
morning with a clang of machinery.

Now an old man sits on the porch;
I can hear it every time he clears his throat . . .

as I stand here, holding the jack,
in the middle of my generation,

by the Lethe of asphalt and dust
and human blood spilled carelessly.

When I look back I see
a field full of grasshoppers. ˞

The hills are hidden with a cloud.
And what pale king sits in the glass?

# The Climate of Paradise

A story about Indians,
the tribe that claimed Mt. Shasta . . .

Five lawyers said, "It's ridiculous!
What possible use can they have for the mountain?"

The interpreter said, "Your Honor,
they say that their gods live there."

\*

How different this is from the Buzzy Schofields,
people I met in Pasadena.

Green lawns, imposing villas—
actually, these are caves inhabited

by Pufendorf's dwarfs and Vico's
Big Feet, the "abandoned by God."

Thought, says Vico, begins in caves—
but not the Buzzy Schofields'.

They're haunted by Red China—
bugles—a sky lit with artillery.

They're terrified they'll be brainwashed.
They can see themselves breaking under torture . . .

"Stop! I'm on your side!
You're making a terrible mistake!"

O even in Paradise
the mind would make its own winter.

# On the Eve

There is something sad about property
where it ends, in California.

A patch of white moving in a crack of the fence . . .
It is the rich widow—
when the dogs howl, she howls like a dog.

        *

At night in San Francisco
the businessmen and drunkards
sink down to the ocean floor.

Their lives are passing.
There is nothing in those depths
but the teeth of sharks and the earbones of whales.

Their lives are passing
slowly under the scrutiny
of goggle eyes, in waves that are vaguely

connected to women.
The women stand up in cages
and do it, their breasts in yellow light.

The businessmen of San Francisco
are mildly exhilarated.
Lifting their heavy arms and feet

they stamp on the ocean floor.
They rise from the ooze of the ocean floor
to the lights that float on the surface.

        *

It is like night in St. Petersburg.
From the Bay a foghorn sounds,

and ships, wrapped in a mist,
creep out with their heavy secrets
to the war "that no one wants."

# The Wall Test

When they say "To the wall!"
and the squad does a right turn,

where do you stand? With the squad
or the man against the wall?

In every case
you find yourself standing against the wall.

# American Dreams

In dreams my life came toward me,
my loves that were slender as gazelles.
But America also dreams. . . .
Dream, you are flying over Russia,
dream, you are falling in Asia.

As I look down the street
on a typical sunny day in California
it is my house that is burning
and my dear ones that lie in the gutter
as the American army enters.

Every day I wake far away
from my life, in a foreign country.
These people are speaking a strange language.
It is strange to me
and strange, I think, even to themselves.

# Doubting

I remember the day I arrived.
In the dawn the land seemed clear
and green and mysterious.

I could see the children of Adam
walking among the haystacks;
then, over the bay, a million sparkling windows.

Make room, let me see too!
Let me see how the counters are served
and move with the crowd's excitement the way it goes.

        *

Since then so much has changed;
as though Washington, Jefferson, Lincoln
were only money and we didn't have it.

As though the terrible saying of Tocqueville
were true: "There is nothing so sordid . . .
as the life of a man in the States."

I would like to destroy myself, or failing that, my neighbors;
to run in the streets, shouting "To the wall!"
I would like to kill a hundred, two hundred, a thousand.

I would like to march, to conquer foreign capitals.

        *

And there's no end, it seems, to the wars of democracy.
What would Washington, what would Jefferson say
of the troops so heavily armed?

They would think they were Hessians,
and ride back into the hills
to find the people that they knew.

        *

I remember another saying:
"It is not the earth, it is not America who is so great . . ."
but "to form individuals."

Every day the soul arrives,
and the light on the mental shore
is still as clear, and still it is mysterious.

I can see each tree distinctly.
I could almost reach out
and touch each house, and the hill blossoming with lilacs.

                    *

I myself am the union of these states,
offering liberty and equality to all.
I share the land equally, I support the arts,

I am developing backward areas.
I look on the negro as myself, I accuse myself
of sociopathic tendencies, I accuse my accusers.

I write encyclopedias and I revise the encyclopedias.
Inside myself there is a record-breaking shot-putter and a track
        team in training.

I send up rockets to the stars.

                    *

Then once more, suddenly, I'm depressed.
Seeming conscious, falling back,
I sway with the soul's convulsion the way it goes;

and learn to be patient with the soul,
breathe in, breathe out,
and to sit by the bed and watch.

# The Pihis

Since first I read in *Zone*
what Apollinaire says of the pihis,
"They have one wing only and fly in a couple"—

I have heard their cries at midnight
and seen the shadows of those passionate
generations of the moon.

# The Photographer

A bearded man seated on a camp-stool—
"The geologist. 1910."

"Staying with friends"—a boy in a straw hat,
on a porch, surrounded with wisteria.

"Noontime"—a view of the Battery
with masts passing over the rooftops.

Then the old horse-cars on Broadway,
people standing around in the garment district.

A high view of Manhattan,
light-shelves with sweeps of shadow.

"Jumpers"—as they come plunging down
their hair bursts into fire.

Then there are photographs of a door knob,
a chair, an unstrung tennis racket.

"Still life. Yes, for a while.
It gives your ideas a connection.

And a beautiful woman yawning
with the back of her hand, like this."

# Simplicity

Climbing the staircase
step by step, feeling my way . . .
I seem to have some trouble with my vision.
The stairs are littered with paper,
eggshells, and other garbage.
Then she comes to the door.
Without eye shadow or lipstick,
with her hair tied in a bun,
in a white dress, she seems ethereal.

"Peter," she says, "how nice!
I thought that you were Albert,
but he hardly ever comes."

She says, "I hope you like my dress.
It's simple. I made it myself.
Nowadays everyone's wearing simple things.
The thing is to be sincere,
and then, when you're tired of something,
you just throw it away."

I'll spare you the description
of all her simple objects:
the bed pushed in one corner;
the naked bulb that hangs
on a wire down from the ceiling
that is stamped out of metal
in squares, each square containing
a pattern of leaves and flowers;
the window with no blinds, admitting
daylight, and the wall
where a stream of yellow ice hangs down
in waves.

            She is saying
"I have sat in this room
all day. There is a time
when you just stare at the wall
all day, and nothing moves.
I can't go on like this any longer,

counting the cracks in the wall,
doting on my buttons."

I seem to be disconnected
from the voice that is speaking
and the sound of the voice that answers.
Things seem to be moving into a vacuum.
I put my head in my hands
and try to concentrate.
But the light shines through my hands,

and then (how shall I put it
exactly?) it's as though she begins
giving off vibrations,
waves of resentment, an aura
of hate you could cut with a knife.
Squirming, looking over her shoulder . . .
Her whole body seems
to shrink, and she speaks in hisses:

"They want to remove my personality.
They're giving me psychotherapy
and *ikebana*, the art of flower arrangement.
Some day, I suppose, I'll be cured,
and then I'll go and live in the suburbs,
doting on dogs and small children."

I go down the stairs, feeling my way
step by step. When I come out,
the light on the snow is blinding.
My shoes crunch on ice and my head
goes floating along, and a voice
from a high, barred window cries
"Write me a poem!"

# Vandergast and the Girl

Vandergast to his neighbors—
the grinding of a garage door
and hiss of gravel in the driveway.

He worked for the insurance company
whose talisman is a phoenix
rising in flames . . . *non omnis moriar*.
From his desk he had a view of the street—

translucent raincoats, and umbrellas,
fluorescent plate-glass windows.
A girl knelt down, arranging
underwear on a female dummy—

sea waves and, on the gale,
Venus, these busy days,
poised in her garter belt and stockings.

    *

The next day he saw her eating
in the restaurant where he usually ate.

Soon they were having lunch together
elsewhere.

    She came from Dallas.
This was only a start, she was ambitious,
twenty-five and still unmarried.
Green eyes with silver spiricles . . .
red hair . . .

    When he held the car door open
her legs were smooth and slender.

"I was wondering,"
she said, "when you'd get round to it,"
and laughed.

    *

Vandergast says he never intended
having an affair.

    And was that what this was?
The names that people give to things . . .

208

What do definitions and divorce-court proceedings
have to do with the breathless reality?

O little lamp at the bedside
with views of Venice and the Bay of Naples,
you understood! *Lactona* toothbrush
and suitcase bought in a hurry,
you were the witnesses of the love
we made in bed together.

*Schrafft's Chocolate Cherries*, surely you remember
when she said she'd be true forever,

and, watching "Dark Storm," we decided
there is something to be said, after all,
for soap opera, "if it makes people happy."

*

The Vandergasts are having some trouble
finding a buyer for their house.

When I go for a walk with Tippy
I pass the unweeded tennis court,
the empty garage, windows heavily shuttered.

Mrs. Vandergast took the children
and went back to her family.

And Vandergast moved to New Jersey,
where he works for an insurance company
whose emblem is the Rock of Gibraltar—
the rest of his life laid out
with the child-support and alimony payments.

As for the girl, she vanished.

Was it worth it? Ask Vandergast.
You'd have to be Vandergast, looking through his eyes
at the house across the street, in Orange, New Jersey.
Maybe on wet days umbrellas and raincoats
set his heart thudding.

                    Maybe
he talks to his pillow, and it whispers,
moving red hair.

In any case, he will soon be forty.

209

# On a Disappearance of the Moon

And I, who used to lie with the moon,
am here in a peat-bog.

With a criminal, an adulterous girl,
and a witch tied down with branches . . .

the glaucous eyeballs gleaming
under the lids, some hairs still on the chin.

# Port Jefferson

My whole life coming to this place,
and understanding it better
maybe for having been born
offshore, and at an early age
left to my own support . . .

I have come where sea and wind,
wave and leaf, are one sighing,
where the house strains at an anchor
and the salt-rose clings and clambers
on the humorous grave.

This is the place, Camerado,
that hides the seabird's nest.
Listening to the distant voices
in summer, a murmur of the sea,
I seem to remember everything.

# Island

Driven by the wind, black billows
surge, and the sand is littered.
Deep, deep in the interior
the temple of the god is hidden.

On slopes overgrown with vines
and thorns, where bees are humming,
with wide, complacent eyes
the wooden face stares calmly.

# A Friend of the Family

Once upon a time in California
the ignorant married the inane
and they lived happily ever after.

But nowadays in the villas
with swimming pools shaped like a kidney
technicians are beating their wives.
They're accusing each other of mental cruelty.

And the children of those parents
are longing for a rustic community.
They want to get back to the good old days.

Coming toward me . . . a slender
sad girl dressed like a sailor . . .
she says, "Do you have any change?"

One morning when the Mother Superior
was opening another can of furniture polish
Cyd ran for the bus
and came to San Francisco.
Now she drifts from pad to pad. "Hey mister,"
she says, "do you have any change?
I mean, for a hamburger. Really."


2

Let Yevtushenko celebrate the construction
of a hydroelectric dam.
For Russians a dam that works is a miracle.

Why should we celebrate it?
There are lights in the mountain states,
sanatoriums, and the music of Beethoven.

Why should we celebrate the construction
of a better bowling alley?
Let Yevtushenko celebrate it.

A hundred, that's how ancient it is
with us, the rapture of material conquest,

democracy "draining a swamp,
turning the course of a river."

The dynamo howls
but the psyche is still, like an Indian.

And those who are still distending the empire
have vanished beyond our sight.
Far from the sense of hearing
and touch, they are merging
with Asia . . .

expanding the war on nature
and the old know-how to Asia.

Nowadays if we want that kind of excitement—
selling beads and whiskey to Indians,
setting up a feed store,
a market in shoes, tires, machine guns,
material ecstasy, money with hands and feet
stacked up like wooden Indians . . .

we must go out to Asia,
or rocketing outward in space.


### 3

What are they doing in Russia
these nights for entertainment?

In our desert where gas pumps shine
the women are changing their hair—
bubbles of gold and magenta . . .
and the young men yearning to be off
full speed . . . like Chichikov

in a troika-rocket, plying
the whip, while stars go flying
(Too bad for the off-beat horse!)

These nights when a space-rocket rises
and everyone sighs "That's Progress!"
I say to myself "That's Chichikov."

As it is right here on earth—
osteopaths on Mars,
actuaries at the Venus-Hilton . . .
Chichikov talking, Chichikov eating,
Chichikov making love.

"Hey Chichikov, where are you going?"

"I'm off to the moon," says Chichikov.

"What will you do when you get there?"

"How do I know?" says Chichikov.


### 4

Andrei, that fish you caught was my uncle.
He lived in Lutsk, not to be confused
with Lodz which is more famous.

When he was twenty he wrote to Chekhov,
and an answer came—"Come to us."
And there it was, signed "Chekhov."

I can see him getting on the train.
It was going to the great city
where Jews had been forbidden.

He went directly to Chekhov's house.
At the door he saw a crowd . . .
they told him that Chekhov had just died.

So he went back to his village.
Years passed . . . he danced at a wedding
and wept at a funeral.

Then, when Hitler sent for the Jews
he said, "And don't forget Isidor . . .
turn left at the pickle-factory."

Andrei, all my life I've been haunted
by Russia—a plain,
a cold wind from the *shtetl*.

215

I can hear the wheels of the train.
It is going to Radom,
it is going to Jerusalem.

In the night where candles shine
I have a luminous family . . .
people with their arms round each other

forever.


5

I can see myself getting off the train.
"Say, can you tell me how to get . . ."

To Chekhov's house perhaps?

That's what everyone wants, and yet
Chekhov was just a man . . . with ideas,
it's true. As I said to him once,
Where on earth do you meet those people?

Vanya who is long-suffering
and Ivanov who is drunk.
And the man, I forget his name,
who thinks everything is forbidden . . .
that you have to have permission
to run, to shout . . .

And the people who say, "Tell us,
what is it you do exactly to justify your existence?"

These idiots rule the world,
Chekhov knew it, and yet
I think he was happy, on his street.
People live here . . . you'd be amazed.

# The Foggy Lane

The houses seem to be floating
in the fog, like lights at sea.

Last summer I came here with a man
who spoke of the ancient Scottish poets—
how they would lie blindfolded,
with a stone placed on the belly,
and so compose their panegyrics . . .
while we, being comfortable, find nothing to praise.

Then I came here with a radical
who said that everything is corrupt;
he wanted to live in a pure world.

And a man from an insurance company
who said that I needed "more protection."

Walking in the foggy lane
I try to keep my attention fixed
on the uneven, muddy surface . . .
the pools made by the rain,
and wheel ruts, and wet leaves,
and the rustling of small animals.

# Sacred Objects

I am taking part in a great experiment—
whether writers can live peacefully in the suburbs
and not be bored to death.

As Whitman said, an American muse
installed amid the kitchen ware.
And we have wonderful household appliances . . .
now tell me about the poets.

Where are your children, Lucina?
Since Eliot died and Pound
has become . . . an authority,
*chef d'école au lieu d'être tout de go,*

I have been listening to the whispers
of U.S. Steel and Anaconda:
"In a little while it will stiffen . . .
blown into the road,

drifting with the foam of chemicals."


2

The light that shines through the *Leaves*
is clear: "to form individuals."

A swamp where the seabirds brood.
When the psyche is still and the soul does nothing,
a Sound, with shining tidal pools and channels.

And the kingdom is within you . . .
the hills and all the streams
running west to the Mississippi.
There the roads are lined with timothy
and the clouds are tangled with the haystacks.

Your loves are a line of birch trees.
When the wind flattens the grass, it
shines, and a butterfly
writes dark lines on the air.

There are your sacred objects,
the wings and gazing eyes
of the life you really have.


3

Where then shall we meet?

Where you left me.

At the drive-in restaurant . . .
the fields on either side covered with stubble,
an odor of gasoline and burning asphalt,
glare on tinted glass, chrome-plated hubcaps and bumpers.

I came out, wiping my hands
on my apron, to take your orders.
Thin hands, streaked with mustard,
give us a hot dog,
give us a Pepsi-Cola.

Listening to the monotonous grasshoppers
for years I have concentrated on the moment.

And at night when the passing headlights hurl
shadows flitting across the wall,
I sit in a window, combing my hair
day in day out.

# Today

On days like this I rush to the pencil sharpener.
The hours pass unnoticed.
On a writing table, in chairs
and corners, in folds of a sunlit curtain,
the touch of a woman lingers.

# Yen Yu

Talking about the *avant-garde* in China
long ago in the 13th century—

"The worst of them," said Yen Yu,
"even scream and growl,
and besides, they use abusive language.
Poetry like this is a disaster."

He said, "Do you see this ant?
Observe, when he meets a procession,
how he pauses, putting out feelers,
and then turns back, in the 'new direction.'
That way he stays out front."

And he said, "Avoid bad poets,
even if they are in the *avant-garde*."

# Love and Poetry

My girl the voluptuous creature
was shaving her legs and saying, "Darling,
if poetry comes not as naturally
as the leaves to a tree
it had better not come at all."

"Och," I said, "and the sorra
be takin your English Johnny!
What, is a poet a thing without brains in its head?
If wishing could do it, I'd compose
poems as grand as physics,
poems founded in botany, psychology, biology,
poems as progressive as the effect
of radiation on a foetus."

She turned on the switch of her razor
and said, "When you talk about poetry
it reminds me of a man in long underwear
doing barbell exercises.
His biceps bulge. In the meantime
outside on the gaslit street
his wife, a voluptuous lady,
elopes with a 'swell' who takes her
to Lindy's for oysters,
from there to the Waldorf, and there
on a bed carved like seashells
they move, while the man with the barbells
by gaslight is marching
and swinging his arms to the tune of the *Washington Post*."

I went to the window. It was night,
and the beautiful moon
was stealing away to meet someone.
The bitches! They want to feel wanted,
and everything else is prose.

# Trasimeno

When Hannibal defeated the Roman army
he stopped at Trasimeno.

That day, and the next, he marched no further.
His tent lay in the moonlight,

his sword shone in the moonlight,
what thought kept him from moving, no one knows.

Stranger, when you go to Rome,
when you have placed your hand in the gargoyle's mouth,

and walked in the alleys . . .
when you have satisfied your hunger for stone,

at night you will return to the trees
and the ways of the barbarians,

hands, eyes, voices, ephemera,
shadows of the African horsemen.

# The Peat-Bog Man

He was one of the consorts of the moon,
and went with the goddess in a cart.

Wherever he went there would be someone,
a few of the last of the old religion.

Here the moon passes behind a cloud.
Fifteen centuries pass,

then one of the bog-peat cutters
digs up the man—with the rope

that ends in a noose at the throat—
a head squashed like a pumpkin.

Yet, there is delicacy in the features
and a peaceful expression . . .

that in Spring the flower comes forth
with a music of pipes and dancing.

# The Silent Piano

We have lived like civilized people.
O ruins, traditions!

And we have seen the barbarians,
breakers of sculpture and glass.

And now we talk of "the inner life,"
and I ask myself, where is it?

Not here, in these streets and houses,
so I think it must be found

in indolence, pure indolence,
an ocean of darkness,

in silence, an arm of the moon,
a hand that enters slowly.

\*

I am reminded of a story
Camus tells, of a man in prison camp.

He had carved a piano keyboard
with a nail on a piece of wood.

And sat there playing the piano.
This music was made entirely of silence.

# Searching for the Ox
## 1976

# Venus in the Tropics

### 1

One morning when I went over to Bournemouth
it was crowded with American sailors—
chubby faces like Jack Oakie
chewing gum and cracking wise.

Pushing each other into the pool,
bellyflopping from the diving boards,
piling on the raft to sink it,
hanging from the rings, then letting go.

Later, when I went into Kingston
to exchange some library books,
they were everywhere, buying souvenirs,
calabash gourds, and necklaces made of seeds.

On Saturday night at the Gaiety
they kept talking and making a noise.
When the management asked them to stop
they told it to get wise, to fly a kite, to scram.

### 2

We drove down to Harbor Street
with Mims ("She isn't your mother.
You ought to call her by some affectionate nickname—
why don't you call her Mims?")

There were two American cruisers,
the turrets and guns distinctly visible,
and some destroyers—I counted four.

The crews were coming ashore in launches.
As each group walked off the dock
we noticed a number of women
wearing high heels. They went up to the sailors
and engaged them in conversation.

"You've seen enough," said Mims.
"In fact, you may have seen too much."

229

She started the Buick, shifting into gear
swiftly with a gloved hand.

She always wore gloves and a broad hat.
To protect her complexion,
she told us. She was extremely sensitive.
All redheaded people were.

"She's a redhead, like Clara Bow,"
our father wrote in his letter.

"The Red Death," said my grandmother
twenty years later, on Eastern Parkway
in Brooklyn. We were talking about my father.
She thought he must have been ill—
not in his right mind—to marry a typist
and leave her practically everything.

How else to explain it, such an intelligent man?


### 3

The American warships left.
Then the *Empress of Britain*
came and stayed for a few days
during which the town was full of tourists.
Then, once more, the harbor was empty.

I sat by the pool at Bournemouth
reading *Typhoon*.
I had the pool all to myself,
the raft, the diving boards, and the rings.
There wasn't a living soul.

Not a voice—just rustling palm leaves
and the tops of the coconuts
moving around in circles.

In the afternoon a wind sprang up,
blowing from the sea to land,
covering the harbor with whitecaps.

It smelled of shells and seaweed,
and something else—perfume.

# Dinner at the Sea-View Inn

### 1

Peter said, "I'd like some air."

"That's a good idea," said Marie's father.
"Why don't you young people go for a walk?"

Marie glanced at her mother.
Something passed between them. A warning.

### 2

When Peter and Marie walked through the dining room
everyone stared.

         *I just think so,*
he reminded himself, and said,
"Fitzgerald says that nobody thinks about us
as much as we think they do."

"Who's he?" said Marie. "Another of your favorite authors?"

### 3

She wanted to know where he was taking her.

"I just had to get out of there.
Wouldn't it be great to hire a taxi
and just keep going?"

              "Why?" said Marie.

"It's a wonderful night."

"I'd rather have my own car," said Marie.

### 4

"I'm getting cold," said Marie.
"How much further are we going?"

"All right," he said.

             And they walked back.

"When I was a child," said Peter,
"I used to think that the waves were cavalry . . .
the way they come in, curling over."

She said, "Is that what you were in,
the calvary?"

He laughed. "Calvary? For Christ's sake . . ."


5

"Did you have a good walk?" said Marie's father.

Marie said something to her mother.

Shortly after, Mr. Shulman ordered the car,
and they all drove back to New York.

They let Peter out in front of his building
on West Eighty-fourth Street, saying goodnight.
All but Marie . . . She still sat stiffly,
unsmiling. She had been offended.


6

Everything was just as he'd left it . . .
the convertible couch,
the reading lamp and chair,
and the stand with the typewriter.

He undressed and went to bed,
and turned out the light.

Lying in bed, hands clasped beneath his head,
listening . . .

to the stopping and starting of traffic
in the street five floors below.
And the opening of the elevator,
and the sound of feet going down the corridor.

# The Psyche of Riverside Drive

The wind was packed with cold.
He pushed against it, over to the Drive
and down a block—watching his step
so as not to slip in the icy slush.

He went through the ritual of entering a building—
speaking on the intercom, the buzzing
and opening of the second door.
He trod the path worn in the carpet
from the entrance to the elevator.

On the right the girl in marble,
Psyche, was in her niche,
her breasts as round, her arms as smooth as ever.
One hand went to her heart; the other
lifted a lamp. It shed no light,
for the globe and the bulb were smashed.
The couch in the opposite wall
where Eros used to lie was empty.

He rang for the elevator.
It came, and he ascended—
smelling some cooking soup or stew,
like the smells that waft through a ship.

And when he walked down the corridor
it seemed that he could feel the engines.
These were cabins, dimly lit.
But all the voyage would be inward.
The people who lived here feared for their lives.

Many had moved to Connecticut.
Those who remained, when you rang,
peered at you through a peephole.
Then the eye withdrew and you heard the bolt drawn back.

It was no grumbling dwarf
or troll who stood in the door,
but Nil Admirari, the Professor.

"Peter," he said, "well well,
I'm glad to see you."

He said, sometimes he thought of Peter
and wondered what he was doing.
Journalism? Well, he smiled,
experience was a hard school . . .
Peter silently finished the sentence:
"but fools will learn in no other."

What would he have? Mrs. Wilson—
for so the Professor referred to his wife—
was, he dared say, making tea.
Or would Peter like something stronger?

He would? Good, so would he.
And he disappeared to find whiskey.
Leaving Peter in excellent company . . .
all *The Great Books*, with the *Syntopicon*,

and the novels of Henry James.
For at that time, after the war,
everybody was either reading Melville
or else they were reading James.
In the words of another famous novelist,
there had been nothing like it
since the craze for table-turning.

Professor Wilson was telling his former student
that the visible world was a dream.

The student thought the Professor was the dream.
How could I, he wondered, ever have listened to this?
He said, "If the world is a dream,
then what shall we say dreams are?
We'll have to think up a new set of words.
For there is a difference between dreaming and waking.
Even if we say that life is a dream

that only feels as though it were real,
the feeling is there. We have to deal with it.
I think," he concluded, "we are playing with words."

"That's it," said the Professor,
"that's just the point."
Then he said, in the special voice
like an Englishman's he used for poetry:
"I have seen violence, I have seen violence.
Give thy heart after letters."

Mrs. Wilson came in.
She looked anemic and had gray hair.

"Margaret," said the Professor,
"you remember Peter.
We are having an interesting discussion."

Mrs. Wilson smiled wanly.
She had seen so many promising students,
and listened to so many interesting discussions.


### 4

He walked over to Broadway,
and kept on walking, though it was cold,
passing the entrance to the subway.
He wanted physical exertion—the solidity
and resonance of the sidewalk under his feet.

The avenue extended—buildings
with windows, rows of blinds and curtains.

He passed the Far East Restaurant,
a laundromat, a liquor store.
A cigar store . . .

Then the Calderon. They were playing
*Amor y Calor*, with Francisca Gonzales.

He looked at the face in the mantilla.
There is always some passionate race
that has just arrived in America.

And a fragrance, *pimienta*,
the wind brings over the sea.

# Lorenzo

## I

In the mornings I would write, sitting on the veranda.
In the afternoons I would go to the village
and then for a swim or a walk.

I was meditating on the embankment
of an abandoned railroad
when a man came by, one of the villagers,
a clerk in string tie and coat.
He struck up a conversation.
When I told him that I wrote,
he said there was an English novelist
named Ascham living in the vicinity.

I had heard of Harry Ascham.
I went to the bookstore and bought one of his works.
This in hand, I approached the villa
where he lived, according to the Frenchman.

## II

Upon my entering
he seized the decanter of whiskey
on the table before him and fled
upstairs, and his wife came down.

I explained—I only wanted to talk—
and she went upstairs. I heard some grumbling,
then he reappeared. In a while,
with drinking whiskey and reminiscing
he warmed. He spoke of Ez
and Tom Eliot
and D. H. Lawrence (Lorenzo).

He spoke of Hilary Thorpe
the poet. Whereupon I put my foot in it,
saying, "Is she still alive?"
not knowing they had once been married.
Ascham looked startled and reached for the decanter
that Sybil, his present wife, kept filled.

He spoke of *The Egoist* and *The Criterion*,
and more about Lawrence . . .
with his TB, the onlie Begetter.
"Did you know," he said, "he lived here, on an island?"


### III

I hired a fisherman's boat,
furrowing the sea, and came
to Lawrence's island.

The path was littered with equipment,
moldy black leather and mess kits
left by the retreating *Wehrmacht*.
On the day of the invasion . . .
thunder . . . the horizon rippling.

The naval guns had fastened on Lawrence's villa
and blown it to bits.
There were only parts of walls
and windows framing the sky.

Little did he care,
being gone to Australia
and America . . . back to Italy
and, finally, to the shades.

Sitting among these stones
I listened to the dry leaves rustling
and thought of a poet's life.
*Genus irritabile vatum.*
Because he longs for Beauty
with man he grows enraged.
Driven here and there . . . If he does find a home,
the world comes along and smashes it.
Just as frequently, he smashes it himself.

Most people can hardly understand it,
content as they are to stay in one place.
Like the cicada, to make one sound repeatedly
all their lives. Monotonous. Like the rasp
of the spring of a watch being wound.

## IV

Ascham said, "Lawrence was a genius
but . . ."
                    Frieda wore long drawers.

When they were living in Taos,
Lawrence dug with his own two hands
a ditch a mile long to bring water.
In the middle of the desert
he made an English garden . . . flowers
such as you still see in Nottingham
outside a miner's cottage.

You could see the drawers hanging on the line
on washdays. Lawrence was a Puritan.
Only an English Puritan
would have written *Lady Chatterley's Lover*.

*He* wouldn't have been such a fool.


## V

I was leaving for Paris
and called to say goodbye.

Ascham had been drinking heavily.
He spoke of his life in California—
writing scripts, he said, for illiterates.
They couldn't even speak their own Yiddish.

He gave me advice: "If you want to be a writer,
write! Don't wait to be asked.
Write reviews. Write articles. Write anything.
And don't think you're a genius."

At the gate looking back
I saw Ascham standing at a window
looking out. He was joined by his wife . . .
as though they were expecting someone

who comes up the path and shouts
"Where are you? Where are you hiding,
Ascham? Come out, you ridiculous man!"

He throws his pack on the table
and puts his boots up on a chair.
He shows you the flower in his buttonhole
he's picked, and wants its name.
You ought to know—it came out of your garden.

He's come a long way
from some far world to this,
bending his neck to the yoke
of local speech and custom . . .
whatever smells of the earth.

He wants to sit up all night talking—
not just about you,
but life. What do you think?
Or has it all been reminiscing?

He wants to hear all the news.
In a few hours he'll be leaving,
resuming his interrupted journey

from the pier-end of the street
to Arcturus and the stars.

# The Stevenson Poster

Talking to someone your own age
who has made a million dollars
you realize that time is passing,
and one thing is sure, you'll never make a million.

He had just bought into a cooperative—
the penthouse, with a magnificent view.
He showed it to me from the patio.
Behind us a roar . . . the housewarming party . . .
the sound poured outward, over the Atlantic.

"Twelve rooms," he had said—
I was impressed.
Especially by one room that had nothing in it
but a tank that glowed deep blue . . .
a tropical aquarium
with coral reefs, places to go in and out.

One fish was adhering to the side of the tank—
"He does the sanitation," said my host.
When I thought of my one and a half rooms
with the Salvation Army furniture,
I could have applied for the job myself.

There were paintings by De Kooning and Hans Hofmann.

In the library, next to a certificate
stating that William Francis Heilbrun
had been "pledged to trout release,"
hung a poster of Adlai Stevenson—
the one where he was running for president
with a hole in the sole of his shoe.

*

Bill and Marion owned a house in East Hampton.
They asked me out one Saturday.
The children had just been given a sailboat—
there was great interest and excitement.
Marion would say, "They're too far out,"

and Bill would tell her not to worry.
Then she went back to *Harper's Bazaar*
and her nails. Whenever I think about her
she is wearing dark glasses and reading *Harper's Bazaar*
or *Vogue*, and polishing her nails.

I would have said they were happy,
but the next time I saw Bill Heilbrun
he and Marion were getting a divorce.

Like other apparently happy couples
they had felt they were "missing out on life."
They kept thinking, Is this all?
Nothing seemed to help, not even analysis,
so they decided to separate, to "start a new life."

They had sold the twelve-room apartment.
The day they moved, he sat down with the movers
and they drank two quarts of whiskey.
They put African drums on the stereo
and went stamping around.
They pried the sanitation expert
off the side of the tank, and flushed him down the toilet.
They tore up the poster of Stevenson
and burned it in the fireplace.

Because the moving men wanted to
and he didn't have the heart to refuse.

# The Hour of Feeling

*Love, now a universal birth,*
*From heart to heart is stealing,*
*From earth to man, from man to earth:*
*—It is the hour of feeling.*
                WORDSWORTH, *To My Sister*

A woman speaks:
"I hear you were in San Francisco.
What did they tell you about me?"

She begins to tremble. I can hear the sound
her elbow made, rapping on the wood.
It was something to see and to hear—
not like the words that pass for life,
things you read about in the papers.

People who read a deeper significance
into everything, every whisper . . .
who believe that a knife crossed with a fork
is a signal . . . by the sheer intensity
of their feeling leave an impression.

And with her, tangled in her hair,
came the atmosphere, four walls,
the avenues of the city
at twilight, the lights going on.

When I left I started to walk.
Once I stopped to look at a window
displaying ice skates and skis.
At another with Florsheim shoes . . .

Thanks to the emotion with which she spoke
I can see half of Manhattan,
the canyons and the avenues.

There are signs high in the air
above Times Square and the vicinity:
a sign for Schenley's Whiskey,
for Admiral Television,
and a sign saying Milltag, whatever that means.

I can see over to Brooklyn and Jersey,
and beyond there are meadows,
and mountains and plains.

# The Sun and the Moon

"If the Sun and Moon should doubt,
They'd immediately go out."

When I try to think what they have in common
I have to say, paranoia.

An unshakable belief in their own importance . . .
They see what they desire.

Certainly, life would be a lot simpler.
You have to be mad, that's the catch.

As it is, I have no one to blame but myself.
I sit down to write . . .

An hour later the table is covered with words.
And then I start crossing them out.

# The Mannequins

Whenever I passed Saks Fifth Avenue
I would stop at a certain window.
They didn't acknowledge my presence—they just stared.

He was sitting in his favorite chair,
smoking a pipe and reading a best seller.
She was standing in front of an easel.

She was finding it easy to paint
by filling in the numbered spaces
with colors. $5.98.

The artificial logs glowed in the fireplace.
Soon it would be Christmas. Santa would come down the chimney,
and they'd give each other presents.

She would give him skis and cuff links.
He would give her a watch with its works exposed,
and a fur coat, and perfume.

Though I knew it was "neurasthenic"
I couldn't help listening to the words
that they said without moving their lips.

# The Middleaged Man

There is a middleaged man, Tim Flanagan,
whom everyone calls "Fireball."
Every night he does the rocket-match trick.
"Ten, nine, eight . . ." On zero
*p f f t*! It flies through the air.

Walking to the subway with Flanagan . . .
He tells me that he lives out in Queens
on Avenue Street, the end of the line.
That he "makes his home" with his sister
who has recently lost her husband.

What is it to me?
Yet I can't help imagining what it would be like
to be Flanagan. Climbing the stairs
and letting himself in . . .
I can see him eating in the kitchen.

He stays up late watching television
From time to time he comes to the window.
At this late hour the streets are deserted.
He looks up and down. He looks right at me,
then he steps back out of sight.

*

Sometimes I wake in the middle of the night
and I have a vision of Flanagan.
He is wearing an old pair of glasses
with a wire bent around the ear
and fastened to the frame with tape.

He is reading a novel by Morley Callaghan.
Whenever I wake he is still there . . .
with his glasses. I wish he would get them fixed.
I cannot sleep as long as there is wire
running from his eye to his ear.

# Newspaper Nights

After midnight when the presses were rolling
we would leave the *Herald Tribune* building
and walk up to Times Square.
The three of us would still be laughing and joking.

I can see a sign that says Schenley.
There are numbers high on a building
telling the time, 12:27,
the temperature, 36.

We have the streets all to ourselves.
There is only the sound of an ambulance or a fire.
There are only the lights that still keep changing
from green to red and back to green in silence.

# Baruch

There is an old folk saying:
"He wishes to study the Torah
but he has a wife and family."
Baruch had a sincere love of learning
but he owned a dress-hat factory.

One night he was in his cart returning
to the village. Falling asleep . . .
All at once he uttered a cry
and snatched up the reins. He flew!
In the distance there was fire
and smoke. It was the factory,
the factory that he owned was burning.

All night it burned, and by daylight
Lev Baruch was a ruined man.
Some said that it was gypsies,
that sparks from their fire set it burning.
Others said, the workers.

But Lev never murmured. To the contrary,
he said, "It is written,
'by night in a pillar of fire.' "
He said, "Every day of my life
I had looked for a sign in that direction.
Now that I have been relieved of my property
I shall give myself to the Word."

And he did from that day on,
reading Rashi and Maimonides.
He was half way over the *Four Mountains*
when one day, in the midst of his studying,
Lev Baruch fell sick and died.
For in Israel it is also written,
"Prophecy is too great a thing for Baruch."

## II

They were lovers of reading in the family.
For instance, Cousin Deborah
who, they said, had read everything . . .
The question was, which would she marry,
Tolstoy or Lermontov or Pushkin?

But her family married her off
to a man from Kiev, a timber merchant
who came from Kiev with a team of horses.
On her wedding day she wept,
and at night when they locked her in
she kicked and beat on the door.
She screamed. So much for the wedding!
As soon as it was daylight, Brodsky—
that was his name—drove back to Kiev
like a man pursued, with his horses.

## III

We have been devoted to words.
Even here in this rich country
Scripture enters and sits down
and lives with us like a relative.
Taking the best chair in the house . . .

His eyes go everywhere, not missing anything.
Wherever his looks go, something ages
and suddenly tears or falls.
Here, a worn place in the carpet,
there, a crack in the wall.

The love of literature goes with us.

On a train approaching midnight
everyone else has climbed into his sarcophagus
except four men playing cards.
There is nothing better than poker—
not for the stakes but the companionship,
trying to outsmart one another.
Taking just one card . . .

I am sitting next to the window,
looking at the lights on the prairie
clicking by. From time to time
two or three will come together
then go wandering off again.

Then I see a face, pale and unearthly,
that is flitting along with the train,
passing over the fields and rooftops,
and I hear a voice out of the past:
"He wishes to study the Torah."

# Mashkin Hill

When Levin mowed Mashkin Hill
there were moments of happy self-forgetfulness.
When he talked to a peasant who believed in God,
Levin realized that he too believed.

In the modern world there aren't any peasants.
They don't cut hay with a scythe,
or the women rake it in windrows.
Now all that work is done by machines.

Now the farmer comes home like anyone
to find that his wife has had her hair done,
and that they're dining by candlelight,
the children having been fed.

And there is no God for Levin
but the quietness of his house.

# Searching for the Ox

I have a friend who works in a mental hospital.
Sometimes he talks of his patients.
There is one, a schizophrenic:
she was born during the Korean War
and raised on an Air Force base.
Then the family moved to La Jolla.
At fourteen she started taking speed
because everyone else was taking it.

Father, I too have my cases:
hands, eyes, voices, ephemera.
They want me to see how they live.
They single me out in a crowd, at a distance,
the one face that will listen
to any incoherent, aimless story.
Then for years they hang around—
"Hey listen!"—tugging at a nerve.
Like the spirits Buddhists call
"hungry ghosts." And when they sense an opening,
rush in. So they are born
and live. So they continue.

There is something in disorder that calls to me.
Out there beyond the harbor
where, every night, the lighthouse
probes the sea with its feathery beam,
something is rising to the surface.
It lies in the darkness breathing,
it floats on the waves regarding
this luminous world,
lights that are shining round the shoreline.
It snorts and splashes,
then rolls its blackness like a tube
back to the bottom.

At dusk when the lamps go on
I have stayed outside and watched
the shadow-life of the interior,

feeling myself apart from it.
A feeling of—as though I were made of glass.
Or the balloon I once saw in Florida
in a swimming pool, with a string
trailing in loops on the surface.
Suddenly the balloon went swivelling
on the water, trying to lift.
Then drifted steadily, being driven
from one side of the pool to the other.


2

There is a light in a window opposite.

All over the world . . . in China
and Africa, they are turning the pages.
All that is necessary is to submit
to engineering, law—one of the disciplines
that, when you submit, drive you forward.

There have been great strides in space.

On a flight leaving Kennedy
I have heard the engineers from IBM
speaking slide rule and doing their calculations.
I saw the first men leave for the moon:
how the rocket clawed at the ground
at first, reluctant to lift;
how it rose, and climbed, and curved,
punching a round, black hole in a cloud.
Before I got back to Orlando
it had been twice round the world.

And still, I must confess,
I fear those *messieurs*, like a peasant
listening to the priests talk Latin.
They will send me off to Heaven
when all I want is to live in the world.


3

The search for the ox continues.
I read in the *Times*, there are young men in Osaka

called Moles. They live underground
in the underground shopping center.
They cut a joint off their little finger,
and they say, "All Al Capone."

I have a friend who has left America—
he finds it more pleasant living in Italy.

O ruins, traditions!
Past a field full of stones,
the ruins of vine-wreathed brickwork,
the road in a soundless march continues
forever into the past.

I have sat in the field full of stones—
stones of an archway, stones
of the columns of the temple,
stones carved S.P.Q.R.,
stones that have been shaped
as women are . . .
Limbs of the gods that have fallen,
too cumbersome to be borne.

By the lake at Trasimeno . . .
If Hannibal had not paused at Trasimeno
the history of the world would have been different.
How so? There would still be a sound
of lapping water, and leaves.


4

"As you have wasted your life here in this corner
you have ruined it all over the world."
This was written by Cavafy who lived in Alexandria.
Alexandria, with blue awnings
that flap in the wind,
sea walls gleaming with reflections.
A steam winch rattles,
an anchor clanks,
smoke drifts over the rooftops,
and at night the lighted streets go sailing.

At night the gods come down—
the earth then seems so pleasant.
They pass through the murmuring crowd.
They are seen in the cafés and restaurants.
They prefer the voice of a child
or the face of a girl to their fame
in their high, cold palaces on Olympus.

In the evening the wind blows from the sea.
The wind rises and winds like a serpent
filling the diaphanous curtains
where the women sit: Mousmé,
Hélène, and the English girl.
When you pass, their lips make a sound,
twittering, like the swallows
in Cyprus that built their nests
in the temple, above the door.
Each one has a sweetheart far away.
They are making their trousseaux;
they don't make love, they knit.

In the bar down the street
a door keeps opening and closing.
Then a pair of heels go hurrying.
In the streets that lead down to the harbor
all night long there are footsteps
and opening doors. It is Eros
Peridromos, who never sleeps till dawn.


### 5

Following in the Way
that "regards sensory experience as relatively unimportant,"
and that aims to teach the follower
"to renounce what one is attached to"—
in spite of this dubious gift
that would end by negating poetry altogether,
in the practice of meditating
on the breath, I find my awareness
of the world—the cry of a bird,
susurrus of tires, the wheezing
of the man in the chair next to me—

has increased. That every sound
falls like a pebble into a well,
sending out ripples that seem to be continuing
through the universe. Sound has a tail
that whips around the corner;
I try not to follow. In any case,
I find I am far more aware
of the present, sensory life.

I seem to understand what the artist
was driving at; every leaf stands clear
and separate. The twig seems to quiver
with intellect. Searching for the ox
I come upon a single hoofprint.
I find the ox, and tame it,
and lead it home. In the next scene
the moon has risen, a cool light.
Both the ox and herdsman vanished.

There is only earth:
in winter laden with snow,
in summer covered with leaves.

# A Donkey Named Hannibal

At times I am visited by a donkey
who was once the great soldier Hannibal.

The reason he didn't take Rome,
he says, was a fear of success.

Now that he has been psychoanalyzed
he would, he is confident, rise to the occasion.

But then he wouldn't be Hannibal.
People would say, "It's a donkey."

So, once more, Hannibal has decided . . .
Moreover, if he succeeded it wouldn't be Rome.

# The Street

Here comes the subway grating fisher
letting down his line through the sidewalk.

Yesterday there was the running man
who sobbed and wept as he ran.

Today there is the subway grating fisher.
Standing as if in thought . . .

He fishes a while. Then winds up the line
and continues to walk, looking down.

# Big Dream, Little Dream

The Elgonyi say, there are big dreams and little dreams.
The little dream is just personal . . .
Sitting in a plane that is flying
too close to the ground. There are wires . . .
on either side there's a wall.

The big dream feels significant.
The big dream is the kind the president has.
He wakes and tells it to the secretary,
together they tell it to the cabinet,
and before you know there is war.

# Before the Poetry Reading

*Composition for Voices, Dutch Banjo, Sick Flute, and a Hair Drum*

### I

This is the poetry reading.
This is the man who is going to give the poetry reading.
He is standing in a street in which the rain is falling
With his suitcase open on the roof of a car for some reason,
And the rain falling into the suitcase,
While the people standing nearby say,
"If you had come on a Monday,
Or a Tuesday, or a Thursday,
If you had come on a Wednesday,
Or on any day but this,
You would have had an audience,
For we here at Quinippiac (Western, or Wretched State U.)
Have wonderful audiences for poetry readings."
By this time he has closed the suitcase
And put it on the back seat, which is empty,
But on the front seat sit Saul Bellow,
James Baldwin, and Uncle Rudy and Fanya.
They are upright, not turning their heads, their fedoras straight on,
For they know where they are going,
And you should know, so they do not deign to answer
When you say, "Where in Hell is this car going?"
Whereupon, with a leap, slamming the door shut,
Taking your suitcase with it, and your Only Available Manuscript,
And leaving you standing there,
The car leaps into the future,
Still raining, in which its taillight disappears.
And a man who is still looking on
With his coat collar turned up, says
"If you had come on a Friday,
A Saturday or a Sunday,
Or if you had come on a Wednesday
Or a Tuesday, there would have been an audience.
For we here at Madagascar
And the University of Lost Causes
Have wonderful audiences for poetry readings."

## II

This is the man who is going to introduce you.
He says, "Could you tell me the names
Of the books you have written.
And is there anything you would like me to say?"

## III

This is the lady who is giving a party for you
After the poetry reading.
She says, "I hope you don't mind, but
I have carefully avoided inviting
Any beautiful, attractive farouche young women,
But the Vicar of Dunstable is coming,
Who is over here this year on an exchange program,
And the Calvinist Spiritual Chorus Society,
And all the members of the Poetry Writing Workshop."

## IV

This is the man who has an announcement to make.
He says, "I have a few announcements.
First, before the poetry reading starts,
If you leave the building and walk rapidly
Ten miles in the opposite direction,
A concert of music and poetry is being given
By Wolfgang Amadeus Mozart and William Shakespeare.
Also, during the intermission
There is time for you to catch the rising
Of the Latter Day Saints at the Day of Judgement.
Directly after the reading,
If you turn left, past the Community Building,
And walk for seventeen miles,
There is tea and little pieces of eraser
Being served in the Gymnasium.
Last week we had a reading by Dante,
And the week before by Sophocles;
A week from tonight, Saint Francis of Assisi will appear in
     person—

But tonight I am happy to introduce
Mister Willoughby, who will make the introduction
Of our guest, Mr. . . ."

# Caviare at the Funeral
## 1980

# Working Late

A light is on in my father's study.
"Still up?" he says, and we are silent,
looking at the harbor lights,
listening to the surf
and the creak of coconut boughs.

He is working late on cases.
No impassioned speech! He argues from evidence,
actually pacing out and measuring,
while the fans revolving on the ceiling
winnow the true from the false.

Once he passed a brass curtain rod
through a head made out of plaster
and showed the jury the angle of fire—
where the murderer must have stood.
For years, all through my childhood,
if I opened a closet . . . bang!
There would be the dead man's head
with a black hole in the forehead.

All the arguing in the world
will not stay the moon.
She has come all the way from Russia
to gaze for a while in a mango tree
and light the wall of a veranda,
before resuming her interrupted journey
beyond the harbor and the lighthouse
at Port Royal, turning away
from land to the open sea.

Yet, nothing in nature changes, from that day to this,
she is still the mother of us all.
I can see the drifting offshore lights,
black posts where the pelicans brood.

And the light that used to shine
at night in my father's study
now shines as late in mine.

# New Lots

On the Sabbath when darkness falls
Pearl Wanateck feeds her hungry ghosts.
Standing before the candles
she prays . . . for all the world
and her relatives over in Russia.

I have seen them in photographs.
One pale rabbinical face . . .
wearing an overcoat that is too long
and yet too short in the sleeves,
standing with his back to a wall.

In the next he has got himself married.
There are two children, a boy and a girl.
This was some time ago. The village
and all who dwelled therein
have been swept from the face of the earth.

## II

The candles cast shadows on the wall.
Hungry ghosts! Not one stalwart tiller of the soil
among them . . . Their unreal occupations!
One works for a theatrical agency,
one at Charles of the Ritz,
one for a stockbrokers' firm.

As though when they left the Old Country
and the streets knee-deep in mud
they swore an oath: Never again!
It would be nothing but steam heat from now on,
and carpeting, wall to wall.
They would take ship to the highest city
and cling there, looking down.

Creeping out at twilight to a restaurant
and a show, then back again.

High above the lighted city
the traffic is hushed.
There are only voices coming from a radio.

It is time now for Jack Benny.

## III

Gefilte fish . . .
carrots and radishes, chicken soup,
boiled chicken and boiled beef . . .
Please pass the horseradish.

Beth is talking . . . about her work at the Ritz.
Yesterday they had a crisis—
Miss Martin's hairdresser called in sick.
She didn't kick up a fuss—
Miss Martin isn't like other celebrities,
though she is a star she's a lady.

Now Dave . . . He works in Whelan's drugstore
on Broadway. They get all sorts of people . . .
actors who are "at liberty,"
shoplifters, people looking for an argument.

He noticed a customer taking lipstick
from the display case and testing it on her arm.
When he went across and spoke to her
"You can kiss my foot!" she cried.
She went hurriedly out. . . .
At the door she turned and stuck out her tongue.

He finishes. No one says anything
until, finally, Grandmother speaks:
"There are a lot of miserable people."

"Yes," someone remarks, "especially in New York."

## IV

Making the return journey by subway . . .
At Forty-Second Street I get off and walk.
I like to look in the windows
at fountain pens and knives,

back-date magazines . . .
the liner in the window of the travel agency
waving good-bye. . . .

But what about the others
who stay?

"A farm was growing in the midst of Paris
and its windows looked out on the Milky Way."
So it is with Dave. After so many years
waiting on customers . . . and his feet hurt . . .
he still thinks it worth it, to have seen
so many famous celebrities, stars of stage and screen.

He once had a conversation with Jolson:
"I have a chiropodist who's a whiz,"
Al told him, and wrote down the address.
"When you're in L.A. look him up,
just tell him Al sent you."

People like the woman in the drugstore . . .
I keep seeing her in a room
in one of the cheap residential hotels
close to Times Square and the theater . . .
seated next to a radiator
in a bathrobe, drying her hair.
Sections of newspaper strewn on the floor . . .

Listening to her breathe . . .
A faucet drips, the radiator hisses,
there is a siren off somewhere.

# Sway

*Swing and sway with Sammy Kaye*

Everyone at Lake Kearney had a nickname:
there was a Bumstead, a Tonto, a Tex,
and, from the slogan of a popular orchestra,
two sisters, Swing and Sway.

Swing jitterbugged, hopping around
on the dance floor, working up a sweat.
Sway was beautiful. My heart went out to her
when she lifted her heavy rack of dishes
and passed through the swinging door.

She was engaged, to an enlisted man
who was stationed at Fort Dix.
He came once or twice on weekends
to see her. I tried talking to him,
but he didn't answer . . . out of stupidity
or dislike, I could not tell which.
In real life he was a furniture salesman.
This was the hero on whom she had chosen
to bestow her affections.

I told her of my ambition:
to write novels conveying the excitement
of life . . . the main building lit up
like a liner on Saturday night;
the sound of the band . . . clarinet,
saxophone, snare drum, piano.
He who would know your heart (America)
must seek it in your songs.

And the contents of your purse . . .
among Kleenex, aspirin,
chewing gum wrappers, combs, et cetera.

"Don't stop," she said, "I'm listening.
Here it is!" flourishing her lighter.

In the afternoon when the dishes were washed
and tables wiped, we rowed out on the lake.
I read aloud . . . *The Duino Elegies,*
while she reclined, one shapely knee up,
trailing a hand in the water.

She had chestnut-colored hair.
Her eyes were changing like the surface
with ripples and the shadows of clouds.

"Beauty," I read to her, "is nothing
but beginning of Terror we're still just able to bear."

*

She came from Jersey, the industrial wasteland
behind which Manhattan suddenly rises.
I could visualize the street where she lived,
and see her muffled against the cold,
in galoshes, trudging to school.
Running about in tennis shoes
all through the summer . . .
I could hear the porch swing squeak
and see into the parlor.
It was divided by a curtain or screen. . . .

"That's it," she said, "all but the screen.
There isn't any."

When she or her sister had a boyfriend
their mother used to stay in the parlor,
pretending to sew, and keeping an eye on them
like Fate.

At night she would lie awake
looking at the sky, spangled over.
Her thoughts were as deep and wide as the sky.
As time went by she had a feeling
of missing out . . . that everything
was happening somewhere else.

Some of the kids she grew up with
went crazy . . . like a car turning over and over.
One of her friends had been beaten
by the police. Some vital fluid
seemed to have gone out of him.
His arms and legs shook. Busted springs.

                    *

She said, "When you're a famous novelist
will you write about me?"

I promised . . . and tried to keep my promise.

Recently, looking for a toolbox,
I came upon some typewritten pages,
all about her. There she is
in a canoe . . . a gust of wind
rustling the leaves along the shore.
Playing tennis, running up and down the baseline.
Down by the boathouse, listening to the orchestra
playing "Sleepy Lagoon."

Then the trouble begins. I can never think of anything
to make the characters do.
We are still sitting in the moonlight
while she finishes her cigarette.
Two people go by, talking in low voices.
A car door slams. Driving off . . .

"I suppose we ought to go,"
I say.
                    And she says, "Not yet."

# On the Ledge

I can see the coast coming near . . .
one of our planes, a Thunderbolt, plunging down
and up again. Seconds later
we heard the rattle of machine guns.

That night we lay among hedgerows.
The night was black. There was thrashing
in a hedgerow, a burst of firing . . .
in the morning, a dead cow.

A plane droned overhead . . .
one of theirs,
diesel, with a rhythmic sound.
Then the bombs came whistling down.


\*


We were strung out on an embankment
side by side in a straight line,
like infantry in World War One
waiting for the whistle to blow.

The Germans knew we were there
and were firing everything they had,
bullets passing right above.
I knew that in a moment the order would come.

There is a page in Dostoevsky
about a man being given the choice
to die, or to stand on a ledge
through all eternity . . .

alive and breathing the air,
looking at the trees, and sky . . .
the wings of a butterfly
as it drifts from stem to stem.

But men who have stepped off the ledge
know all that there is to know:

who survived the Bloody Angle,
Verdun, the first day on the Somme.

As it turned out, we didn't have to.
Instead, they used Typhoons.
They flew over our heads, firing rockets
on the German positions.

So it was easy. We just strolled
over the embankment,
and down the other side,
and across an open field.

Yet, like the man on the ledge,
I still haven't moved . . .
watching an ant
climb a blade of grass and climb back down.

# A Bower of Roses

The mixture of smells—
of Algerian tobacco,
wine barrels, and urine—
I'll never forget it,
he thought, if I live to be a hundred.

And the whores in every street,
and like flies in the bars . . .
Some of them looked familiar:
there was a Simone Simone,
a Veronica.

And some were original,
like the two who stood on a corner,
a brunette with hair like ink
and a platinum blonde,
holding a Great Dane on a leash.

"A monster," said Margot.
"Those two give me the shivers."

The other girls were of the same opinion.
One said, "And, after all,
think what a dog like that must cost to feed."

This was conclusive. They stared out at the street—
there was nothing more to be said.

                    *


When they gave him a pass at the hospital
he would make for the bar in Rue Sainte Apolline
Margot frequented. Sitting in a corner
as though she had been waiting . . .

Like the sweetheart on a postcard
gazing from a bower of roses . . .
"Je t'attends toujours."

For ten thousand francs
she would let him stay the night,

and a thousand for the concièrge.
The maid, too, must have something.

Then, finally, he would be alone with her.
Her face a perfect oval,
a slender neck, brown hair . . .

It surprised him that a girl
who looked delicate in her clothes
was voluptuous when she stood naked.

                    *


He caught up with the division in Germany,
at Dusseldorf, living in houses
a hundred yards from the Rhine.

Now and then a shell flew over.
For every shell Krupp fired
General Motors sent back four.

Division found some cases of beer,
and cigars, and passed them around—
a taste of the luxury
that was coming. The post-war.

One morning they crossed the Rhine.
Then they were marching through villages
where the people stood and stared.
Then they rode in convoys of trucks
on the autobahns. Deeper in.
The areas on the map of Germany
marked with the swastika kept diminishing,
and then, one day, there were none.

                    *


They were ordered back to France,
only sixty kilometers from Paris.

Once more he found himself climbing the stairs.
He knocked, and heard footsteps.
"Who is it?"

The door opened a crack,
then wide, and he was holding her.
"My God," she said, "chéri,
I never thought to see you again."

That night, lying next to her,
he thought about young women
he had known back in the States
who would not let you do anything.
And a song of the first war . . .
"How Are You Going to Keep Them Down on the Farm?
(After They've Seen Paree)."

He supposed this was what life taught you,
that words you thought were a joke,
and applied to someone else,
were real, and applied to you.

# American Classic

It's a classic American scene—
a car stopped off the road
and a man trying to repair it.

The woman who stays in the car
in the classic American scene
stares back at the freeway traffic.

They look surprised, and ashamed
to be so helpless . . .
let down in the middle of the road!

To think that their car would do this!
They look like mountain people
whose son has gone against the law.

But every night they set out food
and the robber goes skulking back to the trees.
That's how it is with the car . . .

it's theirs, they're stuck with it.
Now they know what it's like to sit
and see the world go whizzing by.

In the fume of carbon monoxide and dust
they are not such good Americans
as they thought they were.

The feeling of being left out
through no fault of your own, is common.
That's why I say, an American classic.

# Little Colored Flags

Lines of little colored flags
advertising Foreign Motor Sales . . .
Mario's, the beauty salon,
the hardware store with its display
of wheelbarrows and garbage cans . . .

Most people here are content
to make a decent living.
They take pride in their homes and raising a family.
The women attend meetings of the P.T.A.
Sometimes they drive in to New York
for a day's shopping and the theater.
Their husbands belong to the golf club
or the yacht club.
It makes sense to own a boat if you live in the area.

They go on vacation to Bermuda,
or Europe. Even the Far East.

There aren't too many alternatives.
The couple sitting in the car
will either decide to go home
or to a motel.
Afterwards, they may continue
to see each other, in which case
there will probably be a divorce,
or else they may decide
to stop seeing each other.

Another favorite occupation is gardening . . .
wind rushing in the leaves like a sea.
And the sea itself is there
behind the last house at the end of the street.

# The Beaded Pear

*Kennst du das Land, wo die Zitronen blüh'n?*
GOETHE, *Mignon*

### 1 SHOPPING

Dad in Bermuda shorts, Mom her hair in curlers,
Jimmy, sixteen, and Darlene who is twelve,
are walking through the Smith Haven Mall.

Jimmy needs a new pair of shoes.
In the Mall by actual count
there are twenty-two stores selling shoes:
Wise Shoes, Regal Shoes,
National Shoes, Naturalizer Shoes,
Stride Rite, Selby, Hanover. . . .

Dad has to buy a new lock for the garage,
Mom and Darlene want to look at clothes.
They agree to meet again in an hour
at the fountain.

The Mall is laid out like a cathedral
with two arcades that cross—
Macy's at one end of the main arcade,
Abraham and Straus at the other.
At the junction of transept and nave
there is a circular, sunken area
with stairs where people sit,
mostly teenagers, smoking
and making dates to meet later.
This is what is meant by "at the fountain."

### 2 "WHY DON'T YOU GET TRANSFERRED, DAD?"

One of Jimmy's friends comes by in his car,
and Jimmy goes out. "Be careful,"
Mom says. He has to learn to drive,
but it makes her nervous thinking about it.

Darlene goes over to see Marion
whose father is being transferred

to a new branch of the company
in Houston. "Why don't you get transferred, Dad?"

"I'd like to," he replies.
"I'd also like a million dollars."

This is a constant topic in the family:
where else you would like to live.
Darlene likes California—
"It has beautiful scenery
and you get to meet all the stars."
Mom prefers Arizona, because of a picture
she saw once, in *Good Housekeeping*.
Jimmy doesn't care,
and Dad likes it here. "You can find anything
you want right where you are."
He reminds them of *The Wizard of Oz*,
about happiness, how it is found
right in your own backyard.

Dad's right, Mom always says.
*The Wizard of Oz* is a tradition
in the family. They see it every year.

### 3 The Beaded Pear

The children are home at six,
and they sit down to eat. Mom insists
on their eating together at least once
every week. It keeps the family together.

After helping with the dishes
the children go out again,
and Mom and Dad settle down to watch
"Hollywood Star Time," with Bobby Darin,
Buddy Rich, Laura Nyro,
Judy Collins, and Stevie Wonder.

When this is over he looks in *TV Guide*,
trying to decide
whether to watch "Salty O'Rourke (1945).
A gambler who is readying his horse
for an important race
falls in love with a pretty teacher,"

or, "Delightful family fare,
excellent melodrama of the Mafia."

She has seen enough television
for one night. She gets out the beaded pear
she bought today in the Mall.

A "Special $1.88 do-it-yourself Beaded Pear.
No glueing or sewing required.
Beautiful beaded fruit is easily assembled
using enclosed pins, beads, and decorative material."

She says, "It's not going to be so easy."

"No," he says, "it never is."

She speaks again. "There is a complete series.
Apple, Pear, Banana, Lemon, Orange,
Grapes, Strawberry, Plum, and Lime."

# The Ice Cube Maker

Once the ice was in a tray.
You would hold it under a faucet
till the cubes came unstuck, in a block.
Then you had to run more water over it
until, finally, the cubes came loose.

Later on, there was a handle you lifted,
breaking out the ice cubes.
But still it was a nuisance—
in order to get at one ice cube
you had to melt the whole tray.

Then they invented the ice cube maker
which makes cubes individually,
letting them fall in a container
until it is full, when it stops.
You can just reach in and take ice cubes.

                    *


When her husband came home he saw that she was drunk.
He changed into an old shirt and slacks.
He stared at the screen door in the kitchen . . .
the screen had to be replaced.
He wondered what he was doing. Why fix it?

# Magritte Shaving

How calm the torso of a woman,
like a naked statue . . .
her right leg painted blue,
her left leg colored saffron.
In an alcove . . . The window yields
a view of earth, yellow fields.

            \*

Objects that you may hold loom large:
a wine glass, a shaving brush.
The furniture in the room is small:
a bed, a closet with mirrors . . .
in the room without walls
in the sky full of clouds.

            \*

The sphere, colored orange, floating in space
has a face with fixed brown eyes.
Below the sphere, a shirt with a tie
in a dark, formal suit
stands facing you, close to the parapet
on the edge of the canyon.

# A River Running By

The air was aglimmer, thousands of snowflakes
falling the length of the street.

Five to eight inches, said the radio.
But in the car it was warm;
she had left the engine running
and sat with both hands on the wheel,
her breast and throat like marble
rising from the pool of the dark.

She apologized for the mess:
the litter of junk mail,
an old pair of sneakers,
a suspicious-looking brown paper bag,
and a tennis racket. She had been meaning
to get rid of it. All last summer
she had wondered why her arm hurt,
until a few days ago when she noticed
that the frame was bent.
                              She played tennis
the way she did everything, carelessly.
She hadn't deserved to win,
one woman told her, lacking the right attitude.


                    *


The fallen snow gleamed in the dark
like water. Everything is a flowing,
you have only to flow with it.

If you did, you would live to regret it.
After a while, passion would wear off
and you would still be faced with life,
the same old dull routine.
They would quarrel and make up
regularly. Within a few years
he would grow morose. The trouble with love
is that you have to believe in it.
Like tennis . . . you have to keep it up.

And those who didn't, who remained
on the sofa watching television,
would live to wish that they had.
It was six of one and half a dozen of the other.

"You're serious. What are you thinking?"

That the snow looks like a river.
But there is no river, it is only an idea,
he thought, standing on the edge.

# An Affair in the Country

As he lived on East 82nd Street
and she in Wappingers Falls
he saw more of the road than of her:

Kaufman Carpet
Outlook Realty
Scelfo Realty   Amoco   Color TV

Now and then there would be something out of the ordinary:
X-Rated Dancer
Fabric Gardens   Discount Dog Food

They would meet for a couple of hours
at the Holiday Inn. Then she would have to leave,
and he had to start back.

Speed Zone Ahead
Signal Ahead
Road Narrows
Bridge Out
Yield

# The Old Graveyard at Hauppauge

In Adam's fall we sinned all,
and fell out of Paradise
into mankind—this body of salt
and gathering of the waters,
birth, work, and wedding garment.

But now we are at rest . . .
Aletta and Phebe Almira,
and Augusta Brunce, and the MacCrones . . .
lying in the earth, looking up
at the clouds and drifting trees.

# Unfinished Life

The "villages" begin further out . . .
post office, high school, bank,
built of brick. The state of mind
is Colonial: four white columns
and a watchtower, also white.

Then screens of trees and evergreens
hide the houses, mile on mile.
When the traffic slows to a halt
your eye is attracted to fragments:
a tailpipe, rusted through,
a hubcap, two feet of chain.
Like a battlefield, some great clash of armor . . .

A slice of black rubber
that has crawled out of a crack
and lies on the road like a snake . . .

Not to mention the guardrail
wrenched and twisted out of shape.

You can visualize the accident:
blood seeping in white hair,
turning it cherry-red.

                    *


She said, "I'll be in the garden
if there is anything you need."

He thanked her, and she left,
closing the door silently.
He opened the box and began to read.
Two hours later he was still at it:

"I am sitting with Van Meer,
the old church to our left,
a new 'American' drugstore across the street—
'drugstore publicis' it says repeatedly.
And the Cinema Saint Germain,
showing 'Les Galets d'Etretats' . . .

a woman named Virna Lisi with her mouth open.
A sign saying "Henressy," and the time
in changing numbers.
A 'Brasserie Lipp.'
A pole, painted white, from which a tricolor hangs.
Rue Bonaparte angling left,
making a flatiron with Rue Rennes.
More signs—'Ted Lapidus,' 'Disques Raoul Vidal.' "

The obsession with names and signs,
Peter thought, could be a sign of senility.
Nevertheless, the writing was good,
especially in the places the public would want to read:
his early days in the Village,
then with Norton-Harjes overseas,
and Paris after the war.

The manuscript came to a stop
with a screech of tires, a crash.

A hubcap went rolling in circles,
ringing as it settled.

*

J. B. tapped with a pencil
on the box . . . swung in his chair
and gazed out the window
at the helmeted head of Minerva
in bas-relief on the adjacent building
where none but a head editor
could see it, and the pigeons.
*Sub specie aeternitatis.*

Swung back again . . . "We'll take it,
but you'll have to write a conclusion.
Why do you look," he said, "so dismayed?
You did an outstanding job with *Monica*."

This was a historical romance.
The author, a Southern lady, went insane,
and Peter wrote the missing chapters.

"Couldn't we just end with a note
saying that he left it unfinished?"

"No," said J. B., "I don't think so."
He had the look on his face—inspiration.
There was no arguing with it—
the look he had when he signed the contract
for the cookbook that sold a million.

It was also the look that had turned down
*Cards of Identity* and *Go Tell It on the Mountain*.

He handed the manuscript over . . .
"It needs some final view of things."

*

PROFESSION OF FAITH

As a writer I imagine characters,
giving them definite features
and bodies, a color of hair.
I imagine what they feel
and, finally, make them speak.

Increasingly I have come to believe
that the things we imagine
are not amusements, they are real.

There stands my wife, in the garden
gathering lilacs . . . reaching up,
pulling a branch toward her,
severing the flower with a knife
decisively, like a surgeon.

If I go away, into another country,
all that will remain is a memory.

Once, on a cold winter's night,
driving on a winding road,
fields covered with snow on my left,
on my right a dark body of water,
I conjured up the figure of a man
standing or floating in mid-air.

The things we see and the things we imagine,
afterwards, when you think about them,
are equally composed of words.

It is the words we use, finally,
that matter, if anything does.

*

The last time I saw Van Meer,
if the reader recalls, we were at the Deux Magots
looking across the street
at a *brasserie* and a drugstore,
with people strolling past:
a man with a moustache, wearing a homburg,
the *Légion d'honneur*
in his buttonhole. His wife
in gray, equally distinguished.
Two students, a boy and girl
with dark, nervous eyes.
An old woman, her feet wrapped in rags,
one of the *clochards*
who sleep beneath the bridges.
And the tourists. This year
there is a swarm of Japanese . . .
staring at the people in the café,
the people in the café staring back.
Life, that feeds on the spectacle of itself
to no purpose . . .

He said, "We are, you and I,
in eternity. The difference between us
and them is that we know it."

Shortly after this he died.
But everything is still there.

The shadow of the word
flitting over the scene,
the street and motionless crowd.

# Why Do You Write About Russia?

When I was a child
my mother told stories about the country
she came from. Wolves were howling,
snow fell, the drunken Cossack
shouted in the snow.

Rats prowled the floor of the cellar
where the children slept.
Once, after an illness, she was sent
to Odessa, on the sea. There were battleships
painted white, and ladies and gentlemen
walking the esplanade . . . white naval uniforms
and parasols.

These stories were told
against a background of tropical night . . .
a sea breeze stirring the flowers
that open at dusk, smelling like perfume.
The voice that spoke of freezing cold
itself was warm and infinitely comforting.

So it is with poetry: whatever numbing horrors
it may speak of, the voice itself
tells of love and infinite wonder.

Later, when I came to New York,
I used to go to my grandmother's
in Brooklyn. The names of stations
return in their order like a charm:
Franklin, Nostrand, Kingston.
And members of the family gather:
the three sisters, the one brother,
one of the cousins from Washington,
and myself . . . a "student at Columbia."
But what am I really?

For when my grandmother says,"Eat!
People who work with their heads have to eat more" . . .
Work? Does it deserve a name
so full of seriousness and high purpose?

Gazing across Amsterdam Avenue
at the windows opposite, letting my mind
wander where it will, from the page
to Malaya, or some street in Paris . . .
Drifting smoke. The end will be as fatal
as an opium-eater's dream.

*

The view has changed—to evergreens,
a hedge, and my neighbor's roof.
This too is like a dream, the way we live
with our cars and power mowers . . .
a life that shuns emotion
and the violence that goes with it,
the object being to live quietly
and bring up children to be happy.

Yes, but what are you going to tell them
of what lies ahead?
That the better life seems
the more it goes sour? The child no longer
a child, his happiness all of a sudden
behind him. And he in turn
expected to bring up his children
to be happy . . .

What then do I want?

A life in which there are depths
beyond happiness. As one of my friends,
Grigoryev, says, "Two things
constantly cry out in creation,
the sea and man's soul."

Reaching from where we are
to where we came from . . . *Thalassa!*
a view of the sea.

*

I sit listening to the rasp
of a power saw, the puttering of a motorboat.

The whole meaningless life around me
affirming a positive attitude . . .

When a hat appears, a black felt hat,
gliding along the hedge . . .
then a long, black overcoat
that falls beneath the knee.

He produces a big, purple handkerchief,
brushes off a chair, and sits.

"It's hot," he says, "but I like to walk,
that way you get to see the world.
And so, what are you reading now?"

Chekhov, I tell him.

"Of course. But have you read Leskov?
There are sentences that will stay in your mind
a whole lifetime.
For instance, in the 'Lady Macbeth,'
when the woman says to her lover,
'You couldn't be nearly as desirous
as you say you are, for I heard you singing' . . .
he answers, 'What about gnats?
They sing all their lives, but it's not for joy.' "

So my imaginary friend tells stories
of the same far place the soul comes from.

When I think about Russia
it's not that area of the earth's surface
with Leningrad to the West and Siberia
to the East—I don't know anything
about the continental mass.

It's a sound, such as you hear
in a sea breaking along a shore.

My people came from Russia,
bringing with them nothing
but that sound.

# Typhus

"The whole earth was covered with snow,
and the Snow Queen's sleigh came gliding.
I heard the bells behind me,
and ran, and ran, till I was out of breath."

During the typhus epidemic
she almost died, and would have
but for the woman who lived next door
who cooked for her and watched by the bed.

When she came back to life
and saw herself in a mirror
they had cut off all her hair.
Also, they had burned her clothing,
and her doll, the only one she ever had,
made out of rags and a stick.

Afterwards, they sent her away
to Odessa, to stay with relatives.
The day she was leaving for home
she bought some plums, as a gift
to take back to the family.
They had never seen such plums!
They were in a window, in a basket.
To buy them she spent her last few kopecks.

The journey took three days by train.
It was hot, and the plums were beginning to spoil.
So she ate them . . .
until, finally, all were gone.
The people on the train were astonished.
A child who would eat a plum
and cry . . . then eat another!

                    *


Her sister, Lisa, died of typhus.
The corpse was laid on the floor.

They carried it to the cemetery
in a box, and brought back the box.
"We were poor—a box was worth something."

# The Art of Storytelling

Once upon a time there was a *shocket*,
that is, a kosher butcher,
who went for a walk.

He was standing by the harbor
admiring the ships, all painted white,
when up came three sailors, led by an officer.
"Filth," they said, "who gave you permission?"
and they seized and carried him off.

So he was taken into the navy.
It wasn't a bad life—nothing is.
He learned how to climb and sew,
and to shout "Glad to be of service, Your Excellency!"
He sailed all round the world,
was twice shipwrecked, and had other adventures.
Finally, he made his way back to the village . . .
whereupon he put on his apron, and picked up his knife,
and continued to be a shocket.

At this point, the person telling the story
would say, "This shocket-sailor
was one of our relatives, a distant cousin."

It was always so, they knew they could depend on it.
Even if the story made no sense,
the one in the story would be a relative—
a definite connection with the family.

# The Pawnshop

The first time I saw a pawnshop
I thought, Sheer insanity.
A revolver lying next to a camera,
violins hanging in the air like hams . . .

But in fact there was a reason for everything.

So it is with all these lives:
one is stained from painting with oils;
another has a way of arguing
with a finger along his nose, the Misnagid tradition;
a third sits at a desk made of mahogany.

They are all cunningly displayed
to appeal to someone. Each has its place in the universe.

# Caviare at the Funeral

*This was the village where the deacon*
*ate all the caviare at the funeral.*
CHEKHOV, *In the Ravine*

On the way back from the cemetery
they discussed the funeral arrangements
and the sermon, "such a comfort to the family."

They crowded into the parlor.
It was hot, and voices were beginning to rise.
The deacon found himself beside a plate
heaped with caviare. He helped himself
to a spoonful. Then another.

Suddenly he became aware
that everyone's eyes were upon him,
ruin staring him in the face.
He turned pale. Then tried to carry it off—
one may as well be hanged for a sheep
as a lamb, et cetera.

Meeting their eyes with a stern expression
he took another spoonful,
and another. He finished the plate.

Next morning he was seen at the station
buying a ticket for Kurovskoye,
a village much like ours, only smaller.

# Chocolates

Once some people were visiting Chekhov.
While they made remarks about his genius
the Master fidgeted. Finally
he said, "Do you like chocolates?"

They were astonished, and silent.
He repeated the question,
whereupon one lady plucked up her courage
and murmured shyly, "Yes."

"Tell me," he said, leaning forward,
light glinting from his spectacles,
"what kind? The light, sweet chocolate
or the dark, bitter kind?"

The conversation became general.
They spoke of cherry centers,
of almonds and Brazil nuts.
Losing their inhibitions
they interrupted one another.
For people may not know what they think
about politics in the Balkans,
or the vexed question of men and women,

but everyone has a definite opinion
about the flavor of shredded coconut.
Finally someone spoke of chocolates filled with liqueur,
and everyone, even the author of *Uncle Vanya*,
was at a loss for words.

As they were leaving he stood by the door
and took their hands.
                    In the coach returning to Petersburg
they agreed that it had been a most
*unusual* conversation.

# The Man She Loved

           In the dusk
men with sidelocks, wearing hats
and long black coats walked side by side,
hands clasped behind their backs,
talking Yiddish. It was like being in a foreign country.

The members of the family
arrived one by one . . .
his aunts, his uncle, and his mother
talking about her business
in Venezuela. She had moved to a new building
with enough space and an excellent location.

To their simple, affectionate questions
he returned simple answers.
For how could he explain what it meant to be a writer . . .
a world that was entirely different,
and yet it would include the sofa
and the smell of chicken cooking.

Little did they know as they spoke
that one day they would be immortal
in a novel that commanded the sweep
of Tolstoy, a magnificent creation
that would bring within its compass
offices in Manhattan and jungles
of the Amazon. A grasp of psychology
and sense of the passing of time
that can only be compared to,
without exaggerating, Proust.

The path wound through undergrowth.
Palms rose at an angle from the humid plain.
He passed a hut with chickens and goats . . .
an old man who sat with his back to a wall,
not seeing. A woman came out of a door
and stared after him.
           In the distance
the purple mountains shone, fading
as the heat increased.

"Let me take a look at it,"
said Joey. He took the watch
from Beth, pried open the back,
and laid it on the table before him.
He reached in his jacket
and produced a jeweler's loupe . . .
screwed it into his eye,
and examined the works.
"I can fix it. It only needs an adjustment."

"Are you sure?" said his sister.
"I wouldn't want anything to happen to it.
Jack gave it to me."

The used-car tycoon. But they never married.
"I've got," he said, "a tiger by the tail,"
meaning the used-car business.

Joey stared at her.
"Don't you think I know my business?"

Siblings. Members of the one family,
tied by affection, and doubt . . .
right down to the funeral
when, looking at the face in the box,
you can be sure. "That's real enough."

Spreading her wings at the piano . . .
"The Man I Love." A pleasant voice
but thin.

She traveled to Central America
on the Grace Line, singing with a band.
White boats on a deep blue sea . . .
at night a trail of fireflies.
"Sitting at the Captain's table,"
"Teeing off at the Liguanea Club."

This picture was taken much earlier . . .
three flappers with knee-high skirts.
1921.
They were still living in Delancey Street.

The songs that year were "Say It With Music"
and "If You Would Care For Me."

# Peter

### 1

At the end of the lane a van moving slowly . . .
a single tree like a palm rising above the rest . . .
so this is all there is to it,
your long-sought happiness.

### 2

On winter nights when the moon
hung still behind some scaffolding
you thought, "Like a bird in a cage."
You were always making comparisons . . .
"finding similitudes in dissimilars,"
says Aristotle. A form of insanity . . .
Nothing is ever what it appears to be,
but always like something else.

### 3

One has been flung down with its roots in the air.
Another tilts at an angle.
One has lost a limb in the storm
and stands with a white wound.
And one, covered with vines,
every May puts out a mass of flowers.

### 4

Poetry, says Baudelaire, is melancholy:
the more we desire, the more we shall have to grieve.
Devour a corpse with your eyes; art consists
in the cultivation of pain.
Stupidity reassures you; you do not belong
in a bourgeois establishment, it can never be your home.
Restlessness is a sign of intelligence;
revulsion, the flight of a soul.

# Maria Roberts

In the kingdom of heaven
there is neither past nor future,
but thinking, which is always present.

So it is, at this moment
I am sitting with Maria Roberts
and her young brother, Charles,
in a tram in the South Camp Road.

We are going to the Carib Theater.
But first we shall have to wait
for the tram coming in the other direction.
It seems that we shall spend eternity

staring at the nearest roofs,
trees with the bark shelling off—
eucalyptus—
a hedge that is powdered with dust.

Specks in the sky slowly circling . . .
crows. They seem to hang there.
Like Charley . . . he was shot down
over Germany during the war.

But Maria . . . in the Uffizi
the slender golden Venus,
gray eyes that gaze back at me . . .
must be living still somewhere.

The tram comes around the corner
finally, clanging its gong,
and passes . . . rows of dresses
and trousers and straw hats.

In the last row, the old women
with clay pipes stuck in their teeth
and baskets packed with vegetables
at their feet . . . Going to market.

Then our motorman climbs down
and throws the switch with his pole,

and we're off again, to the theater.
Today they're playing "The Firefly."

In the kingdom of heaven
there is neither past nor future,
but thinking, which is always present:

specks in the sky slowly circling,
a hedge that is covered with dust.

# Armidale

### For George d'Almeida

*Il faut voyager loin en aimant sa maison.*

## AS A MAN WALKS

It's a strange country,
strange for me to have come to.
Cattle standing in a field,
sheep that are motionless
as stones,
the sun sinking in a pile of clouds,
and the eternal flies
getting in your ears and eyes . . .

I suppose you become accustomed.
Mrs. Scully was in her kitchen
entertaining two friends
when one said, "Isn't that a snake?"
and pointed. Sure enough
one was sliding around the divider.
She reached for something, the rolling pin,
and stunned it. Then finished it off
with a hammer.

The green-hide and stringy-bark Australian . . .
my candidate for survival
in the event of fire, flood,
or nuclear explosion.

As a man walks he creates the road he walks on.
All of my life in America
I must have been reeling out of myself
this red dirt, gravel road.

Three boys seated on motorcycles
conferring . . .

                    A little further on,
a beaten-up Holden parked off the road

with two men inside passing the bottle.
Dark-skinned . . . maybe they are aboriginal.

I might have been content to live
in Belle Terre, among houses and lawns,
but inside me are gum trees,
and magpies, cackling and whistling,
and a bush-roaming kangaroo.

## A NUCLEAR FAMILY

The closest I ever came was the zoo.
There was the whole mob lying down
at one end of the compound. And one
really big one, the Old Man,
lying on his side, on his elbow
it looked like. With big hind legs
and tail, and funny drooping forepaws
held high in fly-swatting position.
He seemed asleep, but that was only
the look they all have, sleeping or waking,
the eye concealed by the orb
of the big lid curving down . . .
a look of shyness
or some sweet meditation.

But he's not like that, he's a tough one,
Old Man Kangaroo.
I can see him, after the day's work,
standing in the pub with his mates
talking against the Company.
Then, later, reeling home.
As a man walks he creates the road,
the moon gliding above the housetops
and the shadows.

When he comes in, there's his Missus
in the kitchen, lip curled in scorn.
He decides to brazen it out
(a veteran he of many night sorties) . . .
"Let's ha'e a bit o' dinner, then.
I'm about clammed."
She flares up. "Wheer's my money?

Wheer do I come in?
You've had a good jaunt,
tea waiting and washed up,
then you come crawling in.
You suppose, do you, I'm going to keep house for you
while you make a holiday?
You must think something of yourself."

"Don't be gettin thysen in a roar,"
he says, retreating at once, like a veteran.
He pulls a knotted kerchief out of his moleskin
and unties it with miner's fingers,
clumsy from the pick-work.

"Here's thy blessed money,
thy shillings an thy sixpences,"
pouring it on the table.
Then he reaches a hand to her shoulder,
"Now gie us summat, gie us a kiss."

"Behave thysen," she says, pushing him away,
"the child'll see."

"What child?" He looks around. "What?
Is the dear everywhere? I don't see him.
Are his eyes in the wall?"

"Enow o' thy clatter.
I never seen a rip as th'art.
Shall y'ave your dinner warmed?"

"Ay," he says, "an wi' a smite o' cheese."

## A BUSH BAND

A guitar and drum,
a pole with bottlecaps nailed to it . . .

struck with a piece of wood
it gives off a silvery, joyful sound.

The woman playing the guitar
is sinewy, like the men in the ballad.

Driving their cattle overland
from Broome to Glen Garrick . . .

Cows low, wagon wheels turn,
red dust hangs in the air.

Some give their lives to cattle
and some to the words of a song,

arriving together at Glen Garrick
and at the end of the song.

## DEATH OF THUNDERBOLT

Here he came to a place where two creeks meet,
a gouge in the earth, dry rocks . . .
yet when it rains it can drown you.

Barren and desolate, unless you're an aborigine
when every rock hides the spirit
of one of your departed relatives.

And for those who know the story
there is the figure of Constable Walker
in the saddle, looking down
at Fred Ward, known as Thunderbolt.

Ward is halfway across the creek
on foot, having released his horse
so as to double back to it later.
An old trick of the bushranger . . .
but the constable isn't having any,
he's caught up with Thunderbolt at last.

While parrots flutter in a tree
and a kookaburra laughs like a maniac,
Ward speaks. "Are you a policeman?"
"I am," says Walker. "You surrender."
Then Ward says, "Have you a family?"
to which the constable answers,
"I thought of that before I came here."
And he says again, "You surrender."
"I'll die first," says Ward.

Then the constable, raising his revolver
and shouting "You and I for it!"
struck spur to his horse.

But the beast missed its footing

almost throwing him down.
Ward ran forward and grabbed him by the arm . . .
the constable pressed the muzzle of the revolver
against Ward's body, and fired.
Ward attempted to grasp him again . . .
the constable struck him over the head
with the butt of the revolver. And Ward fell.

Walker stood, to recover his breath,
then lifted Ward under the arms
and half carried, half dragged him onto the bank.
The bushranger's eyes were closed
and there was a stain on his shirt
where the bullet had gone in.

Scarcely believing what had happened,
it all happened so fast,
his own actions appearing like a dream,
the constable mounted and rode back to Uralla.

Where the Coachwood and Cedar Motor Hotel
now stands, at the head of a street
full of shops and offices where men sit
counting money.

But at dusk when the lights shine on
in the little streets and the surrounding hills,
what would the children do without a story?

Getting to his feet, walking back
to his horse that whinnies in a shadow . . .
He climbs in the saddle and rides
into the bush where he still lives.

# Out of Season

Once I stayed at the Grand Hotel
at Beaulieu, on the Mediterranean.
This was in May. A wind blew steadily
from sea to land, banging the shutters.
Now and then a tile would go sailing.

At lunch and dinner we ate fish soup
with big, heavy spoons.
Then there would be fish, then the main course.

At the next table sat an old woman
and her companion, Miss O'Shaughnessy
who was always writing letters
on the desk in the lounge provided for that purpose—
along with copies of *Punch* and *The Tatler*
and an old wind-up Victrola.

There was a businessman from Sweden
and his secretary. She had a stunning figure
on the rocks down by the sea.
She told me, "My name is Helga.
From Vasteras" . . . brushing her hair,
leaning to the right, then to the left.

Also, an Englishman who looked ill
and went for walks by himself.

                    *


I remember a hotel in Kingston
where our mother used to stay
when she came on one of her visits
from America. It was called
the Manor House. There was a long veranda
outside our rooms, and peacocks on the lawn.

We played badminton and golf,
and went swimming at Myrtle Bank.
I did jigsaw puzzles, and water colors,
and read the books she had brought.

In the lounge there were newspapers
from America . . . "Gas House Gang Conquer Giants."
What I liked were the cartoons,
"The Katzenjammer Kids" and "Bringing Up Father."

*

Getting back to Beaulieu . . .
this could have been one of the places
where the Fitzgeralds used to stay—
the bedroom thirty feet across,
a ceiling twelve feet high.
The bathroom, also, was enormous.

A voice would say . . . "Avalon,"
followed by the sound of an orchestra,
and . . . shuffling. This would continue
all night, till two or three,
when the last pair of feet went away.

I was preparing to shave
when an arm came out of the wall.
It was holding a tennis racket.
It waved it twice, moved sideways,
flew up, and vanished through the ceiling.

*

Of course not. Yet, it's weird
how I remember the banging shutters
and the walk to the village
past cork trees and slopes lined with vines.

Narrow, cobbled streets going down to the sea . . .
There would be boats drawn up, and nets
that a fisherman was always mending.

I sat at a table overlooking the Mediterranean.
At the next table sat the Englishman
who looked unwell. I nodded.

He paid for his drink abruptly
and strode away. Terrified
that I might want his company.

At times like this, when I am away from home
or removed in some other way,
it is as though there were another self
that is waiting to find me alone.

Whereupon he steps forward:
"Here we are again, you and me . . .
and sounds . . . the chirping of birds
and whispering of leaves,
the sound of tires passing on the road."

Yes, and images . . . Miss O'Shaughnessy
shouting "Fish soup!" in the old woman's ear.
The businessman from Vasteras
and his girl . . . lying on her side,
the curve of her body
from head to slender feet.

The Englishman walking ahead of me . . .
He has a stick; as he walks
he slashes with it at the reeds
that are growing beside the road.

These things make an unforgettable impression,
as though there were a reason for being here,
in one place rather than another.

# The Mexican Woman

All he needed was fifty cents
to get to a job in Union City.

You wouldn't believe it, he
was in Mexico with Black Jack Pershing.

He lived with a Mexican woman.
Then he followed her, and was wise.

"Baby," he said, "you're a two-timer,
I'm wise to you and the lieutenant."

                    *

I gave him the fifty cents,
but the old man's tale still haunts me.

I know what it's like to serve
in Mexico with Black Jack Pershing.

And to walk in the dust and heat . . .
for I can see her hurrying

to the clay wall where they meet,
and I shall be wise to her and the lieutenant.

313

# Back in the States

It was cold, and all they gave him to wear
was a shirt. And he had malaria.

There was continual singing of hymns—
"Nearer My God to Thee" was a favorite.
And a sound like running water . . .
it took him a while to figure it.

Weeping, coming from the cells
of the men who had been condemned.

Now here he was, back in the States,
idly picking up a magazine,
glancing through the table of contents.

Already becoming like the rest of us.

# People Live Here: Selected Poems 1949–1983
## 1983

# The Fleet for Tsushima

Now we're at sea, like the Russians
In the days of the last Tsars.

The houses of stucco gleaming
Adrift in a fog,

The villas of redwood and glass
And the masts of trees and telephone poles

Are like the fleet for Tsushima;
Now they're mournfully leaving

To sail round the world, to explode
And sink in hideous steam.

Darkening the trees and rooftops
The sailors utter terrible cries.

# The Best Hour
of the Night
1983

# Physical Universe

He woke at five and, unable
to go back to sleep,
went downstairs.

A book was lying on the table
where his son had done his homework.
He took it into the kitchen,
made coffee, poured himself a cup,
and settled down to read.

"There was a local eddy in the swirling gas
of the primordial galaxy,
and a cloud was formed, the protosun,
as wide as the present solar system.

"This contracted. Some of the gas
formed a diffuse, spherical nebula,
a thin disk, that cooled and flattened.
Pulled one way by its own gravity,
the other way by the sun,
it broke, forming smaller clouds,
the protoplanets. Earth
was 2,000 times as wide as it is now."

*The earth was without form, and void,
and darkness was upon the face of the deep.*

\*

"Then the sun began to shine,
dispelling the gases and vapors,
shrinking the planets, melting earth,
separating iron and silicate
to form the core and mantle.
Continents appeared . . ."

history, civilization,
the discovery of America
and the settling of Green Harbor,
bringing us to Tuesday, the seventh of July.

Tuesday, the day they pick up the garbage!
He leapt into action,
took the garbage bag out of its container,
tied it with a twist of wire,
and carried it out to the toolshed,
taking care not to let the screen door slam,
and put it in the large garbage can
that was three-quarters full.
He kept it in the toolshed so the raccoons
couldn't get at it.

He carried the can out to the road,
then went back into the house
and walked around, picking up newspapers
and fliers for: "Thompson Seedless Grapes,
California's finest sweet eating";

"Scott Bathroom Tissue";

"Legislative report from Senator Ken LaValle."

He put all this paper in a box,
and emptied the waste baskets in the two
downstairs bathrooms,
and the basket in the study.

He carried the box out to the road,
taking care not to let the screen door slam,
and placed the box next to the garbage.

Now let the garbage men come!

*

He went back upstairs.
Mary said, "Did you put out the garbage?"
But her eyes were closed.
She was sleeping, yet could speak in her sleep,
ask a question, even answer one.

"Yes," he said, and climbed into bed.
She turned around to face him,
with her eyes still closed.

He thought, perhaps she's an oracle,
speaking from the Collective Unconscious.
He said to her, "Do you agree with Darwin
that people and monkeys have a common ancestor?
Or should we stick to the Bible?"

She said, "Did you take out the garbage?"

"Yes," he said, for the second time.
Then thought about it. Her answer
had something in it of the sublime.
Like a *koan* . . . the kind of irrelevance
a Zen master says to the disciple
who is asking riddles of the universe.

He put his arm around her,
and she continued to breathe evenly
from the depths of sleep.

# How to Live on Long Island

Lilco, $75.17;
Mastercard, $157.89;
Sunmark Industries, $94.03 . . .

Jim is paying his bills.
He writes out a check
and edges it into the envelope
provided by the company.
They always make them too small.

The print in the little box
in the top right corner informs him:
"The Post Office will not deliver
mail without proper postage."
They seem to know that the public
is composed of thieves and half-wits.

He seals the last envelope,
licks a stamp, sticks it on,
and with a feeling of virtue,
a necessary task accomplished,
takes the checks out to the mailbox.

It's a cool, clear night in Fall,
lights flickering through the leaves.
He thinks, all these families
with their situation comedies:
husbands writing checks,
wives studying fund-raising,
children locked in their rooms
listening to the music that appeals to them,
remind me of . . . fireflies
that shine for a night and die.

Of all these similar houses
what shall be left? Not even stones.
One could almost understand the pharaohs
with their pyramids and obelisks.

Every month when he pays his bills
Jim Bandy becomes a philosopher.
The rest of the time he's OK.

Jim has a hobby: fishing.
Last year he flew to Alaska.
Cold the salmon stream,
dark the Douglas firs,
and the pure stars are cold.

A bear came out of the forest.
Jim had two salmon . . . he threw one
but the bear kept coming.
He threw the other . . . it stopped.

The fish that are most memorable
he mounts, with a brass plate
giving the name and place and date:
Chinook Salmon, Red Salmon,
Brown Trout, Grouper,
Barracuda, Hammerhead Shark.

They do a lot of drinking in Alaska.
He saw thirty or forty lying drunk
in the street. And on the plane . . .

They cannot stand living in Alaska,
and he cannot stand Long Island
without flying to Alaska.

# Encounter on the 7:07

He got on at Cold Spring Harbor
and took the seat next to mine—
a man of about forty, with a suntan.

The doctor said, "You need a vacation."
His wife said, "It's an opportunity,
we can visit my sister in Florida."

He played golf every day
and they visited the Everglades.
Trees standing out of the swamp
with moss and vines hanging down,
ripples moving through the water . . .

An alligator is different from a crocodile,
it has a broad head, et cetera.

           \*

There's a car card advertising
"Virginia Slims"—a photographer's model
got up to look like a cowgirl
in boots and a ten-gallon hat.
She's kneeling with a cigarette in her hand
and a smile—in spite of the warning
printed below: "The Surgeon General
has determined that cigarette smoking
is dangerous to your health."

It's the American way
not to be daunted—to smoke cigarettes
and rope cattle all you want.

The man sitting next to me,
whose name is Jerry—Jerry DiBello—
observes that he doesn't smoke cigarettes,
he smokes cigars. "Look at Winston Churchill.
He smoked cigars every day of his life,
and he lived to be over eighty."

*

Wordsworth said that the passions
of people who live in the country
are incorporated with the beautiful
and permanent forms of nature.
In the suburbs they are incorporated
with the things you see from the train:
rows of windshields . . . a factory . . .
a housing development, all the houses
alike, either oblong or square,
like the houses and hotels in a game of *Monopoly*.

A crane, bright orange, bearing the name "Slattery" . . .

"Feldman," a sign says, "Lumber."
A few miles further on . . .
"Feldman, Wood Products."

*

"The Old Coachman Bar and Grill" . . .

His family used to own a restaurant
on 25A . . . DiBello's.

His father came from Genoa
as a seaman, and jumped ship.
In the middle of the night
he went up on deck,
put his shoes and clothes in a bag,
hung it around his neck,
stood on the rail, and jumped.

He swam to shore and hid in the bushes.
The next day he started walking . . .
came to a restaurant and asked for a job
washing dishes. Ten years later
he owned the restaurant.

Jerry didn't go into the business.
He sells automobiles,
has his own Buick-Pontiac showroom.

It's hard to make a living these days.
The government ought to clamp down on the Japanese
flooding the market with their Datsuns.

But I'm not listening—I'm on deck,
looking at the lights of the harbor.
A sea wind fans my cheek.
I hear the waves chuckling
against the side of the ship.

I grasp the iron stanchion,
climb onto the rail,
take a deep breath,
and jump.


                    *


I've brought along *Ulysses*
and am just passing the time of day
with old Troy of the D.M.P.
when be damned but a bloody sweep comes along
and near drives his gear in my eye.

"An *olla putrida* . . .
old fags and cabbage-stumps of quotations,"
said Lawrence. Drawing a circle about himself
and Frieda . . . building an ark,
envisioning the Flood.
But the Flood may be long coming.
In the meantime there is life
every day, and Ennui.

Ever since the middle class
and money have ruled our world
we have been desolate.

                    Like Emma Bovary
in the beech-copse, watching her dog
yapping about, chasing a butterfly.

A feeling of being alone
and separate from the world . . .
"alienation" psychiatrists call it.

Religion would say, this turning away
from life is the life of the soul.

This is why Joyce is such a great writer:
he shows a life of fried bread
and dripping "like a boghole,"
and art that rises out of life
and flies toward the sun,

transfiguring as it flies
the reality . . . Joe Hynes,
Alf Bergan, Bob Doran,
and the saint of the quotidian
himself, Leopold Bloom.

                    *


Jerry has a gang who meet every Saturday
to play poker. For friendly stakes . . .
you can lose twenty or thirty dollars,
that's all. It's the camaraderie
that counts.

                    They talk about the ball game,
politics, tell the latest jokes. . . .

One of the guys sells insurance,
another works at the firehouse.

As if reading my mind . . .
"Don't take us for a bunch of bobos."
There's a chemist who works for Westinghouse,
and a lawyer who's on permanent retainer
with the Long Island Lighting Company.

What, he asks, do I do?

I tell him, and he says, it figures.
The way I was so lost in a book
he could see that I live in a different world.

                    *


In Florida after the storm
the whole area for miles inland

was littered with trees and telephone poles,
wrecked automobiles, houses that had blown down.
There was furniture, chairs, and sofas,
lying in the street, buried in mud.

For days afterwards they were still finding bodies.

When he went for a walk
the shore looked as though it had been swept
with a broom. The sky was clear,
the sun was shining, and the sea was calm.

He felt that he was alone with the universe.
He, Jerry DiBello, was at one with God.

# Damned Suitcase

Her suitcase wasn't in the car,
it was back at the house.
"Everyone," he told her, "above the age of twelve

takes care of her own suitcase.
I can't do everything for you."
She said, "You were loading the car,"

and proceeded to show that Milton
was right: *left to herself, if evil thence ensue,*
*Shee first his weak indulgence will accuse.*

\*

He had already paid for the boat
and a can of worms.
She sat in the stern, he rowed.

"No," he said, "it's impossible.
We have to go back and get your damned suitcase."
"No," she said, "I'll go back. You go on by yourself."

*Thus they in mutual accusation spent*
*The fruitless hours, but neither self-condemning,*
*And of thir vain contést appear'd no end.*

\*

Who would be so foolish as to argue
that his marriage was ordained?
It was an accident, like everything else.

The one he could have truly loved
may have been living in the next street,
but things were arranged so they would never meet.

All our lives depend on some object
that has been misplaced: a handkerchief,
a letter, a goddamned suitcase.

At this point it began to rain.
The lake seethed, the shore was invisible,
they huddled in their raincoats.

It stopped, and the sun shone.
They had drifted close to a rock
covered with purple rhododendrons.

The water next to the boat was clear.
You could see to the bottom,
trout, a foot long, gliding between the reeds.

*

He said, "We'll go back to the house,
and start again. We've lost a day . . .
I don't suppose it makes so much difference."

# Quiet Desperation

At the post office he sees Joe McInnes.
Joe says, "We're having some people over.
It'll be informal. Come as you are."

She is in the middle
of preparing dinner. Tonight
she is trying an experiment:
*Hal Burgonyaual*—Fish-Potato Casserole.
She has cooked and drained the potatoes
and cut the fish in pieces.
Now she has to "mash potatoes,
add butter and hot milk," et cetera.

He relays Joe's invitation.
"No," she says, "not on your life.
Muriel McInnes is no friend of mine."

It appears that she told Muriel
that the Goldins live above their means,
and Muriel told Mary Goldin.

He listens carefully, to get things right.
The feud between the Andersons and the Kellys
began with Ruth Anderson calling Mike Kelly
a reckless driver. Finally
the Andersons had to sell their house and move.

Social life is no joke.
It can be the only life there is.

                    *


In the living room the battle of Iwo Jima
is in progress, watched by his son.
Men are dying on the beach,
pinned down by a machine gun.

The marine carrying the satchel charge
falls. Then Sergeant Stryker
picks up the charge and starts running.

Now you are with the enemy machine gun
firing out of the pillbox
as Stryker comes running,
bullets at his heels kicking up dust.
He makes it to the base of the pillbox,
lights the charge, raises up,
and heaves it through the opening.
The pillbox explodes . . .
the NCO's wave, "Move out!"

And he rises to his feet.
He's seen the movie. Stryker gets killed
just as they're raising the flag.

                    *


A feeling of pressure . . .
There is something that needs to be done
immediately.

            But there is nothing,
only himself. His life is passing,
and afterwards there will be eternity,
silence, and infinite space.

He thinks, "Firewood!"—
and goes to the basement,
takes the Swede-saw off the wall,
and goes outside, to the woodpile.

He carries an armful to the sawhorse
and saws the logs into smaller pieces.
In twenty minutes he has a pile of firewood
cut just the right length.
He carries the cut logs into the house
and arranges them in a neat pile
next to the fireplace.

Then looks around for something else to do,
to relieve the feeling of pressure.

The dog!
He will take the dog for a walk.

*

They make a futile procession . . .
he commanding her to "Heel!"—
she dragging back or straining ahead.

The leaves are turning yellow.
Between the trunks of the trees
the cove is blue, with ripples.
The swans—this year there are seven—
are sailing line astern.

But when you come closer
the rocks above the shore are littered
with daggers of broken glass
where the boys sat on summer nights
and broke beer bottles afterwards.

And the beach is littered, with cans,
containers, heaps of garbage,
newspaper wadded against the sea-wall.
Someone has even dumped a mattress . . .
a definite success!
Some daring guy, some Stryker
in the pickup speeding away.

He cannot bear the sun
going over and going down . . .
the trees and houses vanishing
in quiet every day.

# The Previous Tenant

All that winter it snowed.
The sides of roads were heaped with it.
The nights were quiet. If you stepped outside,
above the dark woods and fields
hung glittering stars and constellations.

My landlord, Stanley, came by now and then
to see how things were going.
I reminded him that the previous tenant
had left boxes full of clothes,
a pair of skis, a rifle,
three shelves of books, and a fishing pole.

All right, he said, he'd get in touch with him.

I said, he must have left in a hurry.

A hurry? Stanley considered.
His eyes gleamed under bushy eyebrows.
Satanic. But I happened to know that Stanley
wouldn't hurt a fly. All that Fall
I'd seen him trying to think of something
to persuade some raccoons to quit the premises—
everything short of a gun.

"McNeil was a bit disorganized,"
he said with a smile.

I asked if he'd like some coffee,
and he said yes. While I was making it
he talked about the previous tenant.


2

A doctor named Hugh McNeil
came on the staff at Mercy Hospital
and bought a house in Point Mercy.

Hugh and Nancy fitted right in . . .
people liked them.
Helen Knox, whose husband was vice-president

336

of the National Maritime Bank,
called on Nancy and invited her
to join the Garden Club.
Then they were asked to join the Golf Club.
(The Levines, on the other hand, hadn't been invited.
After two years of Point Mercy
they sold their house and moved back to Queens.)

The McNeils had children: Tom, fourteen,
and Laurie, nine and a half, nearly ten.
McNeil was one of the fathers on Saturday
dashing about. He drove a green Land Rover
as though he were always on safari
with the children and an Irish setter.

Nancy was nice . . . blonde,
and intelligent—she'd been to Wellesley.
She took on the job of secretary
of the Garden Club, that nobody wanted,
and helped organize the dance at the Yacht Club
on July the Fourth, for Hugh had joined that too.
He bought a "Cal" Thirty Martini-rigged sloop,
and with Tom as crew went sailing.
They came in fifth in the Martha Woodbury
Perpetual Trophy.

           Nancy didn't sail,
it made her seasick. She sat on the patio
with her knitting till the boats hove in sight,
then went down to the basin.

McNeil spoke at village meetings
with moderation and common sense.
Once he argued for retaining
the Latin teacher at the high school.
Latin, he explained, was still useful
for medicine and law, and a foundation
for good English. They heard him out
and voted to let the Latin teacher go
and remodel the gymnasium.
McNeil accepted defeat gracefully.
That was one of the things they liked about him.

The residents of Point Mercy
are proud of their village
with its beautiful homes and gardens
and wild life sanctuary.
Contrary to what people say
about the suburbs, they appreciate culture.
Hugh McNeil was an example . . .
doing the shopping, going to the club,
a man in no way different from themselves,
husband and family man
and good neighbor, who nevertheless spoke Latin.


### 3

Her name was Irene Davis.
Before she married it was Cristiano.
"I met her once," said Helen Knox.
"Harry introduced her to me
at the bank. A dark woman . . .
I think, a touch of the tar brush."

There is no accounting for tastes
observed Sandie Bishop.

The woman's husband was an invalid
and patient of Dr. McNeil.
The green Land Rover had been seen
parked outside the Davises' house
in the afternoon, in the evening,
and once—this was hilarious—the doctor
ran out of gas in that part of town
at three in the morning. He didn't have cash
or credit cards on him, and had to walk
to the nearest open service station.
The attendant let him have a gallon.
"I've been in the same fix," he told McNeil,
"you can pay me some other time."

The attendant talked, and the story
got back to Point Mercy.
"It's a scandal," said Sandie.
"Do you think Nancy knows?"

338

Helen said, "I'm sure she does."

"Someone should have a talk with him,"
Sandie said. She remembered
with some excitement, the occasion
when a resident of Point Mercy
had been thinking of selling his house
to a family that was black.
Every morning he would find garbage
dumped on his lawn. The prospective buyer
received an anonymous letter,
and that was the end of that.

"Let's not be hasty," said Helen
who was president of the Garden Club
and had more experience.
"These things have a way of working themselves out."


4

One day there was a sensation:
Dr. McNeil had been mugged,
beaten and left by the road.

"Mugged?" said the service station attendant.
This was long after the event.

He looked around, but there was no one
in hearing distance, only the dog,
a hound that wandered around
with an infected ear, snapping at flies.
All at once it perked up its ears
and went running. It must have smelled something
mixed with the odor of gasoline
and dust . . . a delirious
fragrance of sensual life.

The attendant leaned closer
and said in a conspiratorial voice,
"He was never mugged.
It was Irene Davis's brothers,
the Cristianos. They had him beat up."

He knew about gangsters. They would beat up a guy
to warn him. The next time it was curtains.


5

So McNeil was in the hospital
with two broken ribs, black eyes,
and a missing tooth.

At the next meeting of the Garden Club
the president said she was as broad-minded
as anyone, but this . . .
here she paused as though it were beneath her
to find words for such low behavior . . .
had brought violence into their midst.

Sandie moved they send a delegation
to the hospital, to demand McNeil's
immediate resignation.

The next day four of the members
called on Dr. Abrahams, chief of staff,
and told him what they wanted.
A short man, with hair on his face,
all the time they were talking he kept turning
from one to the other, and grinning,
like some sort of monkey, Sandie said afterwards.

He thanked them for their concern.
But McNeil's private life—
not that he knew anything about it—
had nothing to do with his work
or his position here at the hospital.
If they would take his advice
they would be careful what they said—
they might find themselves charged
with libel. Speaking, he was sure,
for the entire staff, they were fortunate
to have a surgeon of Hugh McNeil's caliber.

Could he be of service in anything else?
No? Then would they please excuse him . . .
it looked like a busy day.

340

They were halfway to the parking lot.
"What can you expect?" said Helen.
"It was bad enough letting them in,
but to make one chief of staff!"

She knew how to put what they were feeling
into words. This was why
she was president—elected not once
or twice . . . this was her third term in office.


6

Then Nancy sued for divorce.
She had all the evidence she needed:
her husband had been with Irene Davis
in Providence, Rhode Island,
when he was supposed to be in Boston
attending a medical conference.

This was when he moved into the cottage.
It consisted of a small bedroom,
living room, bathroom, kitchen.
Thoreau, who recommends sleeping in the box
railroad workers keep their tools in,
would have found this house commodious.

I could imagine him coming home . . .
putting some fries on a metal sheet
and sliding it into the oven
set at 350 degrees.
Sprinkling a couple of chops
with pepper and garlic.
Deciding which frozen vegetable . . .
say, spinach. Putting the block
in a saucer with water and salt.
Making a salad . . . but this would mean
slicing tomatoes, radishes, scallions,
and washing lettuce. There would be times
when he just couldn't be bothered.

He would have a drink, then a second.
You have to be careful not to make it three
and four. On the other hand

you shouldn't be too careful,
or like Robinson Crusoe you may find yourself
taking pride in the neatness and efficiency
of your domestic arrangements:
all your bowls made out of gourds
lined up on a shelf according to size.
Ditto your spoons.
"A place for everything," you say to the parrot,
"and everything in its place."

Bake the French fries,
boil the frozen vegetable, broil the lamb chops.
You can prepare a nourishing dinner
in twenty minutes, and eat it in five
while reading the *Times* or watching *Charlie's Angels*.

He would watch TV again after dinner.
My God, he'd say to the walls,
it can't be this bad. But it was.
He'd turn it off and pick up a book.
Now that he had plenty of time
he could catch up on the ones he'd missed
when they came out: titles like *Future Shock*
and *The Greening of America*.

Then he was on an express train
racing to the end of the line,
a flash and a moment of excruciating
pain. He was paralyzed,
helpless to move a leg or an arm.

And woke, having fallen asleep
in his chair, to hear the dripping
of snow melting on the roof.

On nights when he couldn't sleep
he'd watch the late late show.
In the dark night of the soul,
says F. Scott Fitzgerald,
it is always three in the morning.
Hemingway says, it isn't so bad . . .
in fact, the best hour of the night
once you've reconciled yourself to insomnia

and stopped worrying about your sins.
And I say that insomnia can be
a positive joy if you're tuned in to *Dames*
or *Gold Diggers of 1933*.
I remember seeing *The Producers*
at three in the morning, and practically
falling out of bed. There are pleasures
known to none but late late movie-goers,
moments of the purest absurdity,
such as, in an otherwise boring movie
starring the Marx Brothers, the "Tenement Symphony"
as sung by Tony Martin.

So there he was, watching Busby Berkeley's
electrically lighted waterfalls,
and the Warner Brothers cuties
viewed from underneath, treading water.

"Ain't we got fun!" shrieked the parrot,
and the goat gave a great bound.


7

Behind the Perry Masons and Agatha Christies
I came across a packet of letters.
It was like being a detective.

When Irene's husband came home
from the hospital, he was confined
to his bed, by doctor's orders.
And McNeil was the doctor.
"Call me at home," said Irene.
"There is no problem about telephone calls."

I copied some of the passages.
They might come in useful. There was an idea for a novel
I'd had for years: *A Bovary of the Sierras* . . .
*The Bovary of Evanston* . . . *The Bovary of Green Harbor*.

There was a paragraph about some flowers
and his cock that might have been conceived
by the author of *Lady Chatterley's Lover*.
It went to show that when an idea

has genuine merit, individuals
far removed in space and time
come upon it independently.

She even knew her Bible:
"When my beloved slipped his hand through the latch-hole
my bowels stirred within me."

Rumor was right. It was her brothers
who had McNeil beaten up.
She told him that he wasn't to see her
ever again. She feared for his life.
"Irene . . . signing off."

But she didn't sign off. Here she was again.
"If you have a new woman in your life
or you've gone back to your wife
I don't want to muck things up.
This is just a peacepipe, kid—
send me a smoke signal
if I'm getting in the way of anything.
Cheerio, Irene."

Then they picked up again where they'd left off.
They had been with each other
yesterday. She could still feel him inside her.

I was beginning to be afraid
for him. For her. For both of them.


                    8

Stanley telephoned to say that McNeil
was coming to pick up his things.

I put the books in cartons,
and piled the cartons and the rest of his things
next to the door: the boxes of clothes,
the skis, the fishing pole,
and the rifle—I was loath to part with it,
the way America was greening.

The next day my predecessor
arrived. A man of forty

with red hair . . . looking slightly angry.
Suspicious. I couldn't put my finger on it.

He was accompanied by a young woman
wearing jeans and a sweater.
She was fair, and had a friendly smile.
"It was good of you to take care
of Hugh's things," she said. "Wasn't it, Hugh?"
"O yes," he said. "Thanks."

I helped them carry things out
to the station wagon. It was snowing again . . .
not flakes, but particles, coming down fast
at an angle, like rain or hail.

They drove away.
She waved. He looked straight ahead.
It appeared he was back on the track
once more, after his derailment.
With a woman of the right kind at his side
to give him a nudge. "Say thanks!"


9

It is always that famous day and year
at the Colony Inn . . . a brick fireplace,
rough-hewn beams, and pewter candlesticks.
From the ceiling hang the flags
of the thirteen original colonies.

The waitresses wear bonnets and muslin gowns
that hang straight from the shoulder
to the floor, leaving their arms and elbows
exposed. Some of the older waitresses
seem to resent being made to dress
like children. Their movements are slow.

One of them arrived finally
to take our order and departed,
moving with slow steps
as befitted an early American.

Maggie said, "Don't look now!
By the window . . . that's Irene Davis,
the woman McNeil had the affair with."

I looked around the room casually
and let my gaze come to rest
on Irene.

They said she was dark. What they hadn't said
was that the darkness, jet-black hair,
was set off by a skin like snow,
like moonlight in a dark field.
Her features were . . . fine. She wouldn't have been
out of place in an Italian villa
with walls five feet thick, and chickens
roosting on the furniture . . . the family
crowded into three rooms upstairs . . .
a *contessa*, married to the invalid son
of impoverished aristocracy.

I wondered what she would have thought
if she'd known I'd read her letters.

There were two people with her:
an old woman with white hair
who looked as though she'd just got off
the boat from Palermo . . .
and a man, he must be Irene's brother . . .
the same black hair and white complexion.
But what in her looked romantic,
in him spelled murder. He was thin
and sinewy . . . wearing a green jacket,
dark green shirt, white tie.

I imagined he was being tolerant
of the restaurant . . . these assholes
with their consommés and casseroles,
their salads consisting of lettuce
and cottage cheese . . . And what was this
for chrissake? Sweet potato
with marshmallow on top . . . you call this food?

But he was on his best behavior.
He didn't pull an automatic

and blow holes through the flags
of the thirteen original colonies.

Irene must have felt me staring.
She turned . . . her eyes met mine
for a few seconds. I had an impression
of . . . defiance. "What do you want?"

I quickly looked away.

10

Maggie was meeting a friend
at three. It was now two-thirty.

So we walked around Island Bay.
The village has been reconstructed
to preserve a Colonial atmosphere.
At the crest of a slope facing the bay
stands the post office. This at least
is authentic. It has four columns,
white of course, and a big golden eagle
above the entrance. On either side
in a crescent, there are shops
with signs lettered in gold:
Optometrist, Pharmacy, Antiques . . .
There's a shop selling Irish linen
and wool. Another selling jewelry
and notions . . . Royal Doulton . . .
little statues of Colonial women
in hoopskirts and wigs,
and the figure of a young girl
in shorts, taking a swing at a golf ball.

The slope goes down to a road.
Between this and the bay
stands a gazebo, an open dome
housing a bust of Hercules.
This, they say, was a ship's figurehead.
All but the bearded head
is a reconstruction . . . some local artist
has added a muscular torso
and draped over one shoulder

the skin of the Nemean lion.
A sillier, more pathetic monster
it would be hard to imagine,
with his doggy nose and wide-open eyes
that seem to say, Look at me.
I never did any harm.

This monument to our culture,
believe it or not, had been vandalized . . .
battered and gashed.
Whoever did it must have used a hammer
or an axe.

I said, "Boys will be boys."

"I'm sure," Maggie said, "it wasn't anyone
from around here."

I wasn't so sure. Our high schools
every year turn out their quota of vandals
and theives. Not to mention illiterates.
You don't have to go into New York City . . .

How, she said, could I be so cynical?

I said, why was it
that when you told the truth
people accused you of being cynical?

We were on our way to having a quarrel.
I didn't want to. I liked Maggie,
with her quizzical way of looking at me,
her air of calm, unclouded judgment,
her mouth that turned down at one corner
when she smiled.

But now she wasn't smiling.
She said, "It's your attitude.
Like what you said in the restaurant
about Hugh McNeil and the Davis woman
being better than the rest of us."

She had her back to the post office.
The wings of the golden eagle
seemed to spring out of her shoulders.

I was filled with a sense of the ridiculous.
She sensed it, and became really angry.
"I know, you prefer vulgar people.
Anyone who tries to be decent and respectable
is either a hypocrite or a fool."

So we had our quarrel.
Then a car drove up and stopped.
It was Helen Knox. She leaned over
and opened the door for Maggie.

"Good afternoon," she said to me,
very cool. I knew what she thought of me
and my writing. A friend told me—
for writers have such friends.

She said, "I thought I ought to read
one of his novels. But I couldn't bring myself
to finish it. Why write about
such ordinary things?

What with chauffeuring the children
and entertaining Harry's friends,
if I find time to read, it has to be something
that takes me out of myself.

You have to be selective—
this is why I read the *New Yorker*, and *Time*,
and subscribe to the Book of the Month."

# The Eleventh Commandment

"Do you know the eleventh commandment?"
Harry asks. I shake my head.
I'm the straight man in these encounters.

"The eleventh commandment,"
he says, "is, 'Don't get caught.' "

Then, as I recall, everyone laughs.

\*

He hands a hundred-dollar bill
to his older boy, to buy fireworks
from a man from New Jersey
who's selling them out of his truck.

Then he and I and the boys
are setting them off. Rockets
go climbing with a whoosh
and bang! The sky above Green Harbor
is lit red, white, and blue.
Bright flares come glimmering down.
People have come out of their houses
and stand in the street, looking up.

A thoroughly illegal operation
that everyone is taking part in . . .
What could be more appropriate
on the Fourth of July? More American?

\*

If you want to accomplish anything
in this world, you can't be too particular.

Ethics are nice to have on a wall, in Latin,
but Latin won't meet a payroll.
And don't give me any of that
about the system. It's the same in Russia.

*

When the financial scandal burst
in the light of the flash he was still smiling,
"confident that he and his partners
would be cleared of all violations"—

kickbacks, misapplication of funds,
conspiracy, fraud, concealment, wire fraud,
falsified books and records, and
interstate transportation of stolen property.

*

"I miss him," she says.

"What makes me sick
is the way everyone's turned against him.

Let me tell you about the people
next door. They're stealing bricks
from a building site. Every night
they drive over and steal some more.
They're making a patio and an outdoor barbecue."

Her younger boy, Kyle, comes over
and stands watchfully in front of me.
He is wearing a spaceman's helmet
and carrying a ray gun or laser.

"Hi there," I say to him.
What else do you say to a six-year-old?

# Periodontics

"Am I hurting you?" says Eubie.
I shake my head, no,
for I've learned not to show pain.
At the school of dental hygiene
where Eubie got her diploma
they teach them not to be put off
by a wince or gathering tear
but to stay on the sensitive spot
and . . . "Festina lente" . . . be thorough.

I try to think of something else . . .
"P.C.," the initials
on the dental unit in front of me.

These were Paula's initials.
The Chapmans lived on Riverside Drive
obliquely across from the sign
for Spry. "Spry for Baking"
it said, and blinked off,
then on again. "For Frying."

The apartment had wall-to-wall carpeting
and dark brown furniture waxed so it shone.
There was a cabinet with glass doors
full of objets d'art: an elephant
carved out of ivory, a wooden Russian doll.
There was an old windup Victrola
with hits from Broadway musicals
and "classics," Gershwin and Tchaikovsky.
A bookcase held *The Wandering Jew* by Eugène Sue.

Mr. Chapman had studied for the Ph.D.
but universities wouldn't hire a Jew
so instead he went into business.

"How are we doing?" says Eubie.
OK, I nod, fine.
I call her my Buchenwald Baby . . .
with her eyes of cornflower blue
that never look into mine

directly, but at some view
slightly to the right or to the left
as she travels with the cavitron.

*

"Oh my God," said Paula,
"he isn't even wearing a tie!"

She looked like a fairy princess
in a bright blue gown
that showed that her breasts
had budded, as Proust would say.

I was wearing a suit
but it was brown and tired.
And I had no tie . . .
I hadn't thought it was required.

"He can wear one of your father's,"
said Mrs. Chapman.

So we went to the prom after all
where Paula danced with everyone else.
As I stood by the wall drinking quantities
of pink lemonade out of paper cups
her laughter rang like a chime of bells.

*

I didn't see her for years
while I was in the army.
Then we made up for lost time
at the movies, in the balcony . . .
on my sofa that converted into a bed . . .
and under the trees—it was summer—
at night on Riverside Drive.

"Spry for Baking" said the sign
shining above the Palisades.
A barge with its warning lights
would be going up the Hudson . . .
the George Washington Bridge
gleaming in the moonlight
against the scudding clouds.

"That's it," said Paula. "There."

                    *

"Are you all right?" says Eubie.
I nod. I'm not going to let on.
Though I brush after every meal,
when she gives me the paper cup
with the liquid that's bright red
and bitter . . . and I have held it in my mouth
for thirty seconds, spat it out,
and rinsed with the mouthwash,
and she hands me the mirror,
there are always some traces
of the plaque that causes decay.

                    *

Mrs. Chapman didn't approve of me.
It took me some time to catch on.
"He's too," she told Paula, "bohemian."

She was saving her precious daughter
for someone able to provide her )
with the better things of life:
wall-to-wall carpeting and dark brown furniture.

Paula wanted to "be in the theater."
So her mother packed her off
to some second-rate school in Boston
where they taught it . . . whatever it was.

Actors, I told her, weren't people.
Like monkeys or parrots
they could repeat sounds and simulate feelings
but had none of their own.

"Don't call me," she said, "I'll call you."

                    *

She was as good as her word . . .
she called, twenty years later.
She had just "winged in" from the Coast
and was staying at a friend's apartment
in Soho. There was a restaurant
right on the corner.

I recognized her at once
though she was wearing a pants suit
and big glasses with rhinestones
and the skin that used to look like
some marvellous tropical fruit
was sallow . . . and the glossy black hair
was still black, but lusterless like ink.

The expressions that used to be endearing . . .
fluttering her eyelashes,
touching her tongue to her top lip,
were like the moving eyelids and mouth
of a doll.

And the shop talk!
She kept dropping names
of people in Hollywood and Beverly Hills
I'd never heard of or wanted to.

I said as much. I could hear myself
sneering, like Diogenes in a washtub.
And what did I have to feel so
superior about?
Where were my screen credits? Did I own a swimming pool?

More to the point . . .
where was the novel I was going to write
that would put Proust in the shade?

                    *


The magic, as they say, was gone,
like a song that used to be on the hit parade.

But there is always a new song,
and some things never change.
Not long ago, visiting a friend
who lives on Riverside Drive
I saw that the sign for Spry
is still there, shining away.

"Spry for Baking." It blinks off
and on again . . . "For Frying."
Then the lights run around in a circle.

# Ed

Ed was in love with a cocktail waitress,
but Ed's family, and his friends,
didn't approve. So he broke it off.

He married a respectable woman
who played the piano. She played well enough
to have been a professional.

Ed's wife left him . . .
Years later, at a family gathering
Ed got drunk and made a fool of himself.

He said, "I should have married Doreen."
"Well," they said, "why didn't you?"

# Bernie

Bernie was part Lithuanian
and part American Indian.
He weighed over two hundred pounds.
My earliest memory of Bernie
has to do with his weight. The university
assigned Bernie, who was some sort of
administrative assistant,
to help me and my wife find a house.

We found a big one—three stories
and a wide porch. Bernie stood on the porch
and jumped, and jumped again,
coming down hard with his cowboy boots.
The floor thundered, but it held.
"That's how you test a house," Bernie said.

We became friends
travelling together to a writers' conference
in Montreal . . . and collapsed,
rolling with laughter, streaming tears,
when the poet from Bengal read his masterpiece,
"Tiki, tiki, parakeety."

We flew to Washington, and marched
in a protest against the war.
Bernie, who was deathly afraid of flying,
got drunk in the airport.
He was also afraid of getting his head busted,
and shook all the way. The peace march
was uneventful where we were.
I walked beside a Benedictine monk
from Minnesota. In other parts of the march
the right things were happening to famous men.

That night Bernie left the hotel
to find a woman.
He came back at two in the morning
completely broke and filled with contrition:
"Why do I do these things to myself?"
He sat on the bed making long-distance calls.

357

Then he said, "Do you have any money?"
I lent him fifteen dollars and he went out again.

He wanted to write, that was why
he was at the university. But he despised
the chickenshit department of English.
He also despised the literary life
in New York, all the *apparatchiki*
named Howard or Norman.

So it came as no surprise
when one day he just suddenly
up and left, with his hound Sylvia
and wife June, whom I've forgotten to mention—
an intelligent, beautiful woman
from a family in Butte that almost died
when she married this part Lithuanian,
part Oglala Sioux,
part pork barrel and part bear.

From time to time one of his books would appear.
Then, as can only happen in America,
he was famous. I heard he was being offered
thirty-thousand-dollar advances.
He went to Hollywood and made a movie.
I saw it . . . it was set in North Dakota.
Two men go hunting in the woods
and have some wild adventures.

When I came home from the movie
I didn't go in, but stood on the porch for a while.
The stars were shining above the trees
and roofs and telephone poles.
Upstairs Alma and the kids were asleep,
safe and snug. I could still see where
Bernie's cowboy heels had hit the floor.
There were half-moon indentations.
The wood was, as they say, distressed.

And so am I. The people I care about
live in different parts of the country
and we no longer keep in touch.

# Elegy for Jake

Taking off the old paint
layer by layer . . .
"Let Zip-Strip do the work."

It is also necessary to scrape.
No one driving by the house
on a quiet Saturday
would know that in the cellar
machine guns, bangalore torpedoes
and eighty-eight-millimeter shells
were going off.
             Or that the shadows
of women were complaining,
"You don't care for anyone but yourself."

Stamping out with a suitcase in one hand,
the reading lamp in the other . . .

Fumes. Open a window
and prop it, the cord being gone,
with *Great Love Stories*, edited by Jake Harmon.

Big Jake, who would be called on to speak
at every important publishers' gathering,
whose sayings were always being quoted
in the *Saturday Review* and the *Times* . . .

Stabbed in the back by his partner.
There was blood on a green, felt-covered table.
He lingered a few years, dying slowly,
moving from place to place.
At the end of a long corridor
the room in which he sat was piled with books.
A window looked across the air shaft
to a ledge where pigeons built their nests.
Here the traffic was hushed,
so that you heard the *rou* and *rou*
of the pigeons. They fluttered,
ruffled, and pecked.

The shadows of their wings
flashed across a sunlit wall.

He had been put in charge of a "cultural series"—
books with a limited audience
but "viable cultural interest."

Why weep for Jake?
Those who live by expense accounts
perish by them. On Madison Avenue
I see in people's faces
marks of some internal bleeding,
fears of slipping, losing one's job.
With one boy at Yale, the other at Deerfield . . .

But before this comes to pass
it is summer. Leafy boughs
of oak and elm are rustling.
Jake is in jeans, with the overnight guest
helping build a split-rail fence.
Jake always makes his weekend guests
help with the chores. It gives them a taste
of living in the country.

He is at the moment of his greatest happiness.
He has just been named Editor of the Year.

Later, on the patio, over frankfurters
and beer—lemonade for the children—
he is talking about Flaubert
to Dick Weinstein, who listens deferentially.
Jake is the intellectual, Dick
the partner who manages finances
at Hyperion Books. Jake and Dick
and their wives are a foursome,
going to restaurants and shows together,
and the wives always on the telephone.

Flaubert, Jake is saying,
was a sadist. Keeping his boots on
while making love to a woman!
He will never forgive him for this.
Besides, Flaubert had no imagination—
you can see it in *Sentimental Education*.

He praises his most recent discovery.
A friend of Adlai Stevenson
has written a novel . . .
"the best thing of its kind
since *War and Peace*. I mean it sincerely."

And he did. That was the secret
of Jake's success. His sincerity.

So one day he went into the boardroom.
Weinstein and the other two partners
were there. And copies of Jake's books—
all the books he'd contracted to publish—
were piled on the table.

               "Mandy,"
Dick said, turning to his secretary,
"you can start." And she began reading
sales figures.

Do you recall *King Richard the Third*
where he keeps the council waiting,
and Hastings is getting nervous
and talks compulsively of Richard,
what a good friend he has been,
and how you can always tell Richard's feelings
by what you see in his face . . .
And the other men seated at the table
start drawing away from Hastings
until they're all at the far end
and he's sitting alone?

So Jake sat, while the figures
went rolling off like doom.
Finally it was finished. "Jake,"
Dick Weinstein said, "you're out."

As I said, he lingered for some years.
The last time I saw him, on Martha's Vineyard,
he had grown a beard . . .
I suppose, to go with the cultural series.

Playing it back. Scraping paint . . .
Shadows flutter and fly across a wall.

# Akhmatova's Husband

Akhmatova's husband, Gumilev,
was a poet and an explorer.
He wrote poems about wild animals
and had fantastic ideas:
a red bird with the head of a girl
and a lost tram that goes wandering . . .

shedding fire "like a storm with dark wings,"
passing over bridges,
by a house with three windows
where a woman he loved once lived,
and, rushing toward him,
two raised hooves and an iron glove.

Gumilev fought in the Great War
with almost incredible valor,
twice winning the Cross of Saint George.
He envisioned a little old man
forging the bullet that would kill him.

It wasn't a German bullet, it was Russian.
Gumilev was killed by his own countrymen
as poets in Russia frequently are.

Everyone talks about Akhmatova
but no one talks about Gumilev.
That wouldn't have mattered to Gumilev.
When the man from the government came to kill him,
"Just give me a cigarette," said Gumilev,
"and let's get it over with."

# Red-Avoiding Pictures

In Japan many years ago
when tides of hate surging to and fro
left heads impaled on fences
and the rivers stained with blood,

painters would work in other colors,
brown, yellow, green and blue . . .
*beni-girai-e.* I too
prefer to make a "red-avoiding picture."

# The Champion Single Sculls

Green leaves lit by the sun,
the rest deep in shadow . . .
a tree is an adequate symbol
of inner or spiritual life.
("The natural object," said E.P.,
"is always the adequate symbol.")

It wasn't just characters . . .
one heard that successful men,
corporation executives, were into
transcendental meditation.
But now they have given it up,
they are into tennis and running.

Though I have prayed with Eliot,
"Teach us to sit still,"
this could be laziness,
and life could be very dull.
Besides, the wicked are not still,
they are sharpening a sword.

                    *


Stillness, said a picture,
is not being immobile,
but a clear separation
of the self from its surroundings
while taking part (we must take part,
how else are we to live?)

"Max Schmitt in a Single Scull" . . .
A river with iron bridges . . .
Schmitt is resting on his oars,
looking toward the observer,
"both in and out of the game."
Rowing! This is what I have to practice.

# A Fine Day for Straw Hats

He bought an old ship's lifeboat,
gave it an engine,
and built on a roof extending
from the stern to the bow.
It looked like a house, but it ran.

He christened it *Seahawk*,
and we travelled across the harbor
to Port Royal . . . sand and coconuts,
a few houses and huts,
and a low wall with embrasures
for cannon. This was Fort Charles
where Nelson used to stand
gazing at the sun and the pelicans.

And there were streets and ruins
in the weedy ooze below . . .
the pirate town that vanished
in an earthquake long ago.

*

The trip back was monotonous,
the fan of the wake subsiding
in foam, the thrumming of the engine . . .

When a ship had anchored in the harbor
we would go slowly around it
and read the name on the stern.

There used to be white steamers,
the Grace Line, sailing the Caribbean.
We saw the *Empress of Britain*,

and once, the battle cruiser *Rodney*.
I imagined the big guns firing,
the flame and smoke of battle,
ships sliding beneath the waves.

*

One Christmas we were in the *Seahawk*
off Kingston. An excursion launch

was setting out, crowded with passengers,
straw hats and gaily colored frocks.

I gazed away, to the Palisades . . .
behind them a sleeve of smoke
unravelling . . . a ship at sea.

When I looked again the excursion launch
had vanished. There were only seagulls,
and a confused murmur
coming from the people on shore.

We steered where the launch had been
and circled. The garden boy,
who also served as an able seaman,
fished up something with the boat hook . . .
a man's straw hat.
He placed it on the seat and we stared at it.

Next day's *Gleaner* carried the story:
the launch had capsized,
more than forty were feared drowned.

I don't think I was frightened
so much as appalled. That this could happen
at Christmas, on a calm sea . . .

Nothing, the sea whispers, is certain.

                    *

Reflections of the harbor
flit on walls. On the veranda
leaves are rustling. In the afternoon
a breeze springs up, driving whitecaps
into shore. The tops of the palms
thrash and swerve.

Sea clouds are drifting over.
Years, and a house seems to drift
and hills appear to have moved.

But memory is secure,
it is anchored with a chain.
Nothing short of a hurricane
could ever tear it loose.

# A Remembrance of Things Past

For a long time I stayed in bed
reading Proust, in the two Random House volumes
wherever they happened to fall open.

For the truth is not in chronology,
day turning to dusk in the street outside.
Real time is inside one's head . . .
the white hawthorn blossoms at Combray,
Balbec by the foam-lined sea.

The doctor, a friend of Cottard's,
diagnosed my condition as "neurasthenic."

And if you aren't rich, and don't have servants . . .
So I got out of bed finally,
and carried Proust kicking down the hall
to the incinerator, and dropped him in.

A heavy thud. A second . . .

                    *


The man who stopped me on the bank of the Seine
to tell his story, was a Frenchman
of middle age. He had obviously had a few.

"You are," he said, "American,
and would never have heard of Proust.
Monsieur Proust was a writer, a great man.
I was his companion and chauffeur.

"One day when I entered the apartment
I put a hand on the wall.
For days and months afterwards
Monsieur Proust would go over to the wall
to see if there was still a mark."

He delivered this as proof.
There, you see,
that is what it is to have genius!

He is wearing a cloth cap, the sign
of the European "man of forty."
He has a moustache, a pink complexion
heightened with wine.

He invites me to come and visit him—
he owns a hotel—and talk about Proust.

I can see the published interview,
maybe even a *New Yorker* "profile."

But what would this have to do
with Proust . . . a rushing of traffic
through the streets of Manhattan at dusk,
windows suddenly lighting up,
the radio in the next apartment,
murmur of voices and clatter of dishes?

I thanked him, and did not go.

# The Gardener

She is on her knees pulling weeds.
Her soul is desirous, it longs for cucumbers
and melons if they will grow.

When the earth was without form, and void,
and darkness upon the face of the deep,
the soul was born, a piece of the void

broken off . . . the winged Psyche,
Desire, who is always wandering
over these lawns and between these houses.

She clings for a while
to a flower or a book, then launches
once more her little sail.

# Reflections in a Spa

The walls are lined with mirrors,
doubling their images, front and back.
You see yourself receding in a tunnel.

The man on the adjacent bicycle
speaks: "Whakunam?"
Finally I understand: he has no voice box.
"Whakunam?" means "What's your name?"
"Amjaw"—"I am George."

There are impressive physical specimens:
body builders, weight lifters
with limbs of oak, bellies ridged like washboards.
On the other hand, some whose doctors
have said, "Exercise, or else!"

And some like George, and a night watchman
whose legs are withered and walks
dragging each foot across the floor,
like a "partially destroyed insect"—
the cripple Doyle in *Miss Lonelyhearts*.

The time will pass more easily
thinking about *Miss Lonelyhearts*.
Without fiction life would be hell.

I feel like a disembodied spirit.
Who is that balding middle-aged man
in the mirror, pedalling away from me?
Strange, the back of one's own head
and body growing small.

# In Otto's Basement

At the meeting of the village board
last night in Otto's basement
when they were discussing a building violation—
Why hasn't the building inspector reported?
The village lawyer is waiting to hear from him.
The inspector has to be told to "get off the pot"—
a picture drifted into my mind
from some Latin American country,
of men tied to posts, about to be shot.
Or perhaps it was Africa, or Afghanistan.

So we endure it. This is what Jefferson
and Lincoln had to endure,
sitting and listening to people
argue . . . the cost of conversion from oil to coal
and the statement by the tree-trimming committee.
If you want to know what freedom cost
look for us here, under the linoleum.
Dig between the end of the table
and the wall of some brown material
grained like wood, with imitation knotholes.

# In a Time of Peace

He changes dollars into francs
and walks, from Rue de Rivoli
almost to the Arc de Triomphe.

He sits at a sidewalk café
and looks at the ones who are passing.
Then goes to a restaurant
and a show.

       Someone told him the Crazy Horse
is the place to go, "un spectacle de deux heures"
you can understand "if you're Javanese,
dead drunk, or mentally retarded."
There are sketches, stripteases:
blonde Solange, black Marianne,
Ingrid with her boots and whip . . .
and who can forget Duzia,
"the most wanted girl in Europe"?

The chorus in the entr'actes
jump and squeal. Imagining
their own nudity is driving them mad.

After the show he chooses to walk.
The lamps in leafy avenues
shining on monuments and statues . . .

        *

A sea of amethyst is breaking
along two miles of beach umbrellas . . .
the car parks, red roofs
of the bathing establishments,
Lidino, Antaura . . . advertisements
for Stock, Coca-Cola,
"tutte le Sera DISCOTECA."

A child on the crowded sand
is playing with a new toy.

It hurls an object into the air,
a parachute opens, it descends . . .
homunculus, a little plastic man
returning from Outer Space.

Some day we may have to live there,
but for the present life consists
of sex . . . all the beautiful bodies
that you see on the beach;
food—there are dozens of places,
ranging from the ice-cream parlor
to Tito's—Ristorante Tito del Molo;
things to buy: Galletti for handbags,
Timpano for a lighter;
and entertainment: the Cinema Odeon,
the bar with pinball machines.
There is even a Sauna Finlandese.

At night the promenade glitters,
loud music fills the air.
Not good music . . . but it doesn't matter
to the families with small children
or to the lovers.

# The Unwritten Poem

You will never write the poem about Italy.
What Socrates said about love
is true of poetry—where is it?
Not in beautiful faces and distant scenery
but the one who writes and loves.

In your life here, on this street
where the houses from the outside
are all alike, and so are the people.
Inside, the furniture is dreadful—
floc on the walls, and huge color television.

To love and write unrequited
is the poet's fate. Here you'll need
all your ardor and ingenuity.
This is the front and these are the heroes—
a life beginning with "Hi!" and ending with "So long!"

You must rise to the sound of the alarm
and march to catch the 6:20—
watch as they ascend the station platform
and, grasping briefcases, pass beyond your gaze
and hurl themselves into the flames.

# Index of Titles

Adam Yankev, 194
Aegean, 61
Affair in the Country, An, 286
After Midnight, 182
Akhmatova's Husband, 362
Allan Fox, 3
American Classic, 277
American Dreams, 201
American in the Thieves' Market, An, 95
American Poetry, 154
American Preludes, 56
Arm in Arm, 9
Armidale, 305
Arrivistes, The, 26
Art of Storytelling, The, 296
As Birds are Fitted to the Boughs, 48
Ash and the Oak, The, 55


Back in the States, 314
Baruch, 248
Battle, The, 53
Beaded Pear, The, 279
Before the Poetry Reading, 260
Bernie, 357
Big Dream, Little Dream, 259
Birch, 141
Bird, The, 125
Boarder, The, 92
Bower of Roses, A, 274


Carentan O Carentan, 23
Caviare at the Funeral, 298
Champion Single Sculls, The, 364
Chocolates, 299
Climate of Paradise, 198
Columbus, 172
Côte d'Azur, 98
Country House, The, 191
Cradle Trap, The, 143

375

Damned Suitcase, 331
Dinner at the Sea-View Inn, 231
Donkey Named Hannibal, A, 257
Doubting, 202
Dream of Governors, A, 84
Dvonya, 187

Early in the Morning, 60
Ed, 356
Elegy for Jake, 359
Eleventh Commandment, The, 350
Encounter on the 7:07, 326

Farm in Minnesota, A, 159
Fine Day for Straw Hats, A, 365
Fleet for Tsushima, The, 317
Flight to Cytherea, The, 88
Foggy Lane, The, 217
Friend of the Family, A, 213
Frogs, 151

Gardener, The, 369
Good News of Death, 67
Goodnight, The, 131
Green Shepherd, The, 81

Heroes, The, 54
Hot Night on Water Street, 91
Hour of Feeling, The, 242
How to Live on Long Island, 324

I Dreamed that in a City Dark as Paris, 83
Ice Cube Maker, The, 282
In a Time of Peace, 372
In California, 135
In Otto's Basement, 371
In the Suburbs, 136
Indian Country, 196
Inner Part, The, 155
Invitation to a Quiet Life, 11
Isidor, 193
Island, 212
Islanders, 63

Jamaica, 5

Laertes in Paris, 18
Laurel Tree, The, 174
Lazarus Convalescent, 10
Lines Written Near San Francisco, 165
Little Colored Flags, 278
Lorenzo, 236
Love and Poetry, 222
Love, My Machine, 160
Lover's Ghost, The, 130
Luminous Night, 183

Magritte Shaving, 283
Man She Loved, The, 300
Man Who Married Magdelene, The, 50
Mannequins, The, 245
Maria Roberts, 303
Mashkin Hill, 251
Memories of a Lost War, 52
Mexican Woman, The, 313
Meyer, 190
Middleaged Man, The, 246
Mississippi, 62
Morning Light, The, 142
Moving the Walls, 147
Music in Venice, 96
My Father in the Night Commanding No, 152

New Lines for Cuscuscaraway and Mirza Murad Ali Beg, 146
New Lots, 266
Newspaper Nights, 247
Night in Odessa, A, 192

Old Graveyard at Happauge, The, 287
Old Soldier, 124
On a Disappearance of the Moon, 210
On the Eve, 199
On the Lawn at the Villa, 156
On the Ledge, 272
Orpheus in America, 93
Orpheus in the Underworld, 86
Out of Season, 310
Outward, 179

Pacific Ideas—A Letter to Walt Whitman, 164
Pawnshop, The, 297
Peat-Bog Man, The, 224
Periodontics, 352
Peter, 302
Photographer, The, 205
Physical Universe, 321
Pihis, The, 204
Port Jefferson, 211
Previous Tenant, The, 336
Protestant, The, 17
Psyche of Riverside Drive, The, 233

Quiet Desperation, 333

Red-Avoiding Pictures, 363
Redwoods, The, 137
Reflections in a Spa, 370
Remembrance of Things Past, A, 367
Resistance, 22
Riders Held Back, The, 157
River Running By, A, 284
Roll, 8
Room and Board, 16
Runner, The, 100

Sacred Objects, 218
Searching for the Ox, 252
Silent Generation, The, 129
Silent Piano, The, 225
Simplicity, 206
Son of the Romanovs, A, 188
Song: "Rough Winds Do Shake the Darling Buds of May", 25
Stevenson Poster, The, 240
Story about Chicken Soup, A, 144
Street, The, 258
Stumpfoot on 42nd Street, 180
Summer Morning, 140
Summer Storm, 13
Sun and the Moon, The, 244
Sway, 269

There Is, 138
Things, 177

To the Western World, 90
Today, 220
Trasimeno, 223
Troika, The, 145
True Weather for Women, The, 47
Typhus, 295

Unfinished Life, 288
Union Barge on Staten Island, The, 171
Unwritten Poem, The, 374

Vandergast and the Girl, 208
Venus in the Tropics, 229

Wall Test, The, 200
Walt Whitman at Bear Mountain, 162
Warrior's Return, The, 7
West, 59
Why Do You Write about Russia?, 292
Why This?, 15
Wind, Clouds, and the Delicate Curve of the World, 161
Window, The, 51
Witty War, A, 14
Woman Too Well Remembered, A, 49
Working Late, 265

Yen Yu, 221
Yes Yes, 21

# Index of First Lines

A bearded man seated on a camp-stool—    205
A bell and rattle,    143
A dream of battle on a windy night    124
After midnight when the presses were rolling    247
After the show the silver stars were out    3
A hot midsummer night on Water Street—    91
Akhmatova's husband, Gumilev,    362
A light is on in my father's study.    265
All he needed was fifty cents    313
All that winter it snowed.    336
A man stood in the laurel tree    177
"Am I hurting you?" says Eubie.    352
And I, who used to lie with the moon,    210
"And the condemned man ate a hearty meal,"    100
A Negro sprouts from the pavement like an asparagus.    180
Arm in arm in the Dutch dyke    9
As birds are fitted to the boughs    48
As he lived on East 82nd Street    286
A siren sang, and Europe turned away    90
As I walked with my friend,    172
A story about Indians,    198
At the end of the lane a van moving slowly . . .    302
At the meeting of the village board    371
At the post office he sees Joe McInnes.    333
At times I am visited by a donkey    257
A woman speaks:    242

Bernie was part Lithuanian    357
Birch tree, you remind me    141

Christian says, "You know, it's Paradise,"    98
Climbing the staircase    206
Come, Amaryllis, let us go    11

Dad in Bermuda shorts, Mom her hair in curlers,    279
Decades of disaster, a deluge . . .    18
Dismiss the instruments that for your pleasure    96
"Do you know the eleventh commandment?"    350
Driven by the wind, black billows    212

Early in the morning    60
Ed was in love with a cocktail waitress,    356
Everyone at Lake Kearney had a nickname:    269

Far from your crumpled mountains, plains that vultures ponder,    5
For a long time I stayed in bed    367

Grandfather puts down his tea glass    192
Green leaves lit by the sun,    364

Having put on new fashions, she demands    49
He bought an old ship's lifeboat,    365
He changes dollars into francs    372
He got on at Cold Spring Harbor    326
Helmet and rifle, pack and overcoat    53
Here are your meadows, Love, as wide as heaven,    93
Here comes the subway grating fisher    258
Here I am, troubling the dream coast    135
Here sit a shepherd and a shepherdess,    81
Her suitcase wasn't in the car,    331
*He stood still by her bed*    131
He was one of the consorts of the moon,    224
He woke at five and, unable    321
How calm the torso of a woman,    283

I am taking part in a great experiment—    218
I can see the coast coming near . . .    272
*"Ich wünscht', ich wäre ein Vöglein,"*    125
I dreamed of war-heroes, of wounded war-heroes    54
I dreamed that in a city dark as Paris    83
I fear the headless man    130
"If the Sun and Moon should doubt,    244
I have a friend who works in a mental hospital.    252
I love the dark race of poets,    183
In Adam's fall we sinned all,    287
In dreams my life came toward me,    201
In Italy the dead have all the passion.    95
In Japan many years ago    363
In my grandmother's house there was always chicken soup    144
In Russia there were three students,    190
In that so sudden summer storm they tried    13
In the clear light that confuses everything    174
In the dusk    300
In the kingdom of heaven    303

In the morning light a line    142
In the mornings I would write, sitting on the veranda.    236
In the town of Odessa    187
I remember the day I arrived.    202
Isidor was always plotting    193
It's a classic American scene—    277
It's a strange country,    305
It was cold, and all they gave him to wear    314
I wake and feel the city trembling.    165

Lilco, $75.17;    324
Lines of little colored flags    278
Look! From my window there's a view    138
Love, my machine,    160

Memory rising in the steppes    194
Mountains are moving, rivers    137
My father in the night commanding No    152
My girl the voluptuous creature    222
My whole life coming to this place,    211

Neither on horseback nor seated,    162
Night, dark night, night of my distress—    86
Now we're at sea, like the Russians    317

O amiable prospect!    146
Oh strict society, bright town    7
Oh, we loved long and happily, God knows!    14
Once I stayed at the Grand Hotel    310
Once some people were visiting Chekhov.    299
Once the ice was in a tray.    282
Once upon a time in California    213
Once upon a time there was a *shocket*,    296
On days like this I rush to the pencil-sharpener.    220
One morning, as we travelled in the fields    157
One morning when I went over to Bournemouth    229
On the lawn at the villa—    156
On the Sabbath when darkness falls    266
On the way back from the cemetery    298
On the winding road under the white Alp    22
On US 101    59

Peter said, "I'd like some air."    231
Poetry has no place, still you must choose    63

She is on her knees pulling weeds.    369
Since first I read in *Zone*    204
Stop and tell us, Mister Cuddy, where at such a pace you're going.    67

Taking off the old paint    359
Talking about the *avant-garde* in China    221
Talking to someone your own age    240
The air was aglimmer, thousands of snowflakes    284
The corn rows walk the earth,    159
The crazy pier, a roof of splinters    171
The curtained windows of New York    16
The dark streets are deserted,    182
The Elgonyi say, there are big dreams and little dreams.    259
The first time I saw a pawnshop    297
The gray roof of Saint Germain,    17
The guns know what is what, but underneath    52
The houses seem to be floating    217
The Knight from the world's end    83
The man who married Magdalene    49
The mixture of smells—    274
The prince of Monaco    147
There are designs in curtains that can kill,    88
There are whole blocks in New York    140
There is a middleaged man, Tim Flanagan,    246
There is an old folk saying:    248
There is something sad about property    199
There's no way out.    136
These are the evening hours and he walks    10
These are the houses of the poor—    51
The staff slips from the hand    179
The storm broke, and it rained,    151
The sun hangs from a crag    21
The time is after dinner. Cigarettes    92
The "villages" begin further out . . .    288
The walls are lined with mirrors,    370
The white moon    26
"The whole earth was covered with snow,    295
The wind was packed with cold.    233
This is Avram the cello-mender,    188
This isle hath many goodly woods and deer,    56
This is the poetry reading.    260
This prairie light . . . I see    196

Trees in the old days used to stand    23
Troika, troika! The snow moon    145

Vandergast to his neighbors—    208

We have lived like civilized people.    225
Whatever it is, it must have    154
What, my friends! Dead only two years and already dumb?    8
Whenever I passed Saks Fifth Avenue    245
When Hannibal defeated the Roman army    223
When Hitler was the Devil    129
When I was a child    292
When Levin mowed Mashkin Hill    251
When men discovered freedom first    55
When the schooners were drifting    164
When they had won the war    155
When they say "To the wall!"    200
When we went down the river on a raft    62
Where only flowers fret    61
Why this?    15
Wind, clouds, and the delicate curve of the world    161

You always know what to expect    191
Young women in their April moodiness    47
You will never write the poem about Italy.    374